BEANS - SOAK & COOK

WOK

P.27. BANANA BREAD - (9x5 LOAF PAN)

P.39 MEX BAKE CHICKEN - BEANS

P.53 PASTA TOPPINGS

P.54 RICE TOPPINGS

P.55 POTATO TOPPINGS - P.13

P.56 HUMMUS

P.61. BEANS X

P.60. CHICKEN - EGGS

P.66. FISH

Nancy Clark's

Food Guide for Marathoners

Tips for Everyday Champions

Meyer & Meyer Sport

DEDICATION

I dedicate this book to the marathoners who give of their time and energy to raise money for important causes; they help make the world a better place. May the information in this book help these everyday champions enjoy high energy, good health and "smooth running" throughout their training and the marathon itself.

British Library Cataloguing in Publication Data
A catalogue record for this book is available from the British Library

Nancy Clark's Food Guide for Marathoners
Oxford: Meyer & Meyer Sport (UK) Ltd., 2007
ISBN 978-1-84126-206-2

© 2007 by Meyer & Meyer Sport (UK) Ltd.
Aachen, Adelaide, Auckland, Budapest, Graz, Johannesburg,
New York, Olten (CH), Oxford, Singapore, Toronto
Member of the World
Sports Publishers' Association (WSPA)
www.w-s-p-a.org
Printed and bound by: B.O.S.S Druck und Medien GmbH, Germany
ISBN 978-1-84126-206-2
E-Mail: verlag@m-m-sports.com
www.m-m-sports.com

Contents

Foreword 6
Preface 7
Acknowledgments 8

Section I. Everyday Eating for Marathoners
1. . . . Day-to-Day Eating for Health and High Energy 9
2. . . Breakfast: The Meal of Champions 23
3. . . How to Manage Lunch, Snacks, and Dinner 29
4. . . Vitamins and Supplements for Marathoners 41

Section II. Balancing Carbs, Protein, Fats, and Fluids
5. . . . Carbohydrate Confusion 53
6. . . Protein for Marathoners 57
7. . . . Fats and Your Sports Diet 67
8. . . Water and Sports Drinks 75

Section III. Fueling Long Walks and Runs
9. . . Fueling Before You Exercise 81
10. . . Foods and Fluids During Long Walks and Runs 89
11. . . Recovering from Exhaustive Training 97
12. . . Marathon Week: Nutrition Preparations 105
13. . . Tips for the Traveling Marathoner 115

Section IV. Weight and Marathoners
14. . . Calculating Your Calorie Needs 121
15. . . Weight Reduction for Marathoners 127
16. . . Dieting Gone Awry 137
17. . . How to Gain Weight Healthfully 145

Afterword 149
Additional Resources 150
Recommended Books 151
Internet Resources 152
Selected References 153
Index 155
Photo & Illustration Credits 168

Foreword

During my 40 + years of running and 30 + years of coaching, I've come to appreciate the role of nutrition in fitness, sport, and long-term health. I've consulted with a number of nutritional experts during this period. I've not found anyone more knowledgeable or more experienced in working with runners than Nancy Clark. When the right foods are eaten, at the right time, recovery time is reduced, energy is sustained, and the muscles work better. An even greater psychological boost occurs due to proper ingestion of fluids and blood sugar boosting foods. Nancy's proven advice will also bestow an added level of confidence, which reduces stress and improves performance.

Nancy's advice is based upon solid research. She studies the new findings and knows the trends. For decades, she has advised thousands of runners and solved thousands of nutritional problems. I believe that Nancy's articles are so popular because she covers the issues thoroughly but explains the concepts in easy-to-understand language. She tells you what she knows will work, from a deep well of experience and intelligence.

Nancy is a runner and a marathoner. She's put her advice to the test, and fine-tuned it on the roads.I highly recommend this book.

Jeff Galloway

Preface

"I've got my training down, but nutrition is my missing link" reported David, a novice marathoner who recognized he could have far better stamina and endurance if he could only manage to eat better. David's story is familiar to many of my clients who have the dedication to train but just cannot seem to muster the same dedication to stick to their desired nutrition program. Somehow "eating well" can become difficult as marathoners spend more and more time training, stretching and recovering from their long walks or runs.

And then there are the novice marathon finishers who want to do yet another marathon so they have the chance to learn from their mistakes. As Jessica, a two-time marathoner reported, "I started running a year ago. I ran the L.A. marathon in 5:19, and I learned a lot from that first marathon. I next ran the San Francisco Marathon in 4:52. I was on pace for a 4:30 marathon, but I hit the wall at mile 20 ... I know I didn't eat right. So now, I want to know:

- Am I eating the right foods on a daily basis?
- What should I eat for snacks?
- What can I do about the hunger horrors at 4:00 in the afternoon?
- What should I eat during my long runs?
- What's the best way to carbo-load?
- Would I be a better runner if I were lighter?
- If so, how can I lose weight and still have energy to exercise?"

Like many marathoners, Jessica's workday was a marathon in itself! She started her day with an early morning run (5:30 to 6:30 a.m.) and ended with rushing home from work to cook dinner for her family. She barely grabbed breakfast and lunch, so as soon as she walked in the door to her kitchen, she started devouring almonds by the handful and grapes by the bunches. She'd hoped that running would result in the loss of her undesired body fat, but the fat failed to "melt away," much to her dismay.

Jessica came to me frustrated, filled with questions, and eager to learn how to eat better, fuel her muscles optimally, and enjoy not only higher energy but also better training runs and a faster third marathon. I assured her I could help her reach her goal. I reminded Jessica—and all aspiring marathoners such as yourself—that, while training is an important part of your marathon preparation, proper fueling is equally important. If you don't make the time to eat wisely and well, you might as well hang up your dream of flying through the marathon with energy to spare! But, if you take to heart the information in this *Food Guide for Marathoners* and practice eating wisely (as well as training wisely), you'll be far more likely to have a satisfying marathon experience.

With best wishes for miles of high energy, smiles and wonderful memories,

Nancy Clark, Ms, RD
Certified Specialist in Sports Dietetics (CSSD)
Healthworks Fitness Center
1300 Boylston Street
Chestnut Hill, MA, 02467
www.nancyclarkrd.com

Acknowledgements

With sincere thanks and appreciation to:

Hans Meyer, Thomas Stengel and Kathrin Albrecht for their publishing help. Kerstin Vonderbank for designing a nice-looking book.

Photographers Bob Fitzgerald, Tommy Owens, Tom Dooley, Bruce Zavodny, Jim Newsom, Will Arts, Kate Carter

Larry Armstrong, PhD for granting permission to use the Urine Color Chart.

My husband John McGrath, for his ever-available help, support and love.

My children, John Michael and Mary, for their interest and abundant suggestions.

My running buddies, Jean Smith and Catherine Farrell, for keeping me on my toes.

My clients, many of whom are marathoners, for sharing their experiences and teaching me how to better help other marathoners with similar struggles.

The many participants in the Team in Training Marathon training programs as well as other marathon training programs. They are inspirational!

Chapter 1

Day-to-Day Eating for Health and High Energy

> **"** I try to live by the 80/20 rule: 80 percent of the time I eat nutritious food; 20 percent of the time I have fun foods as a reward for my hard training. The 20 percent includes chocolate, beer, onion rings, blue cheese, doughnuts, and ice cream.
>
> Earl Fenstermacher,
> Seattle, WA **"**

Food is one of life's pleasures. Food not only fuels you for your marathon training program, but also for this marathon called life. Before you started training for a marathon, you may have gotten away with eating on the run and grabbing hit or miss meals. But now that you have embarked upon your marathon training program, food has become an essential source of fuel that can help you train at your best, stay healthy, and complete long runs at your best—to say nothing about enjoying the marathon itself. But you may be wondering: How can I manage to find the time and energy to fuel myself properly?

Fueling yourself well on a daily basis requires management skills. You need to learn how to find time to food shop so you'll have wholesome sports foods available, as well as to find time to fuel up and refuel at the right times. In this chapter, I'll share with you the basic tips about how to eat well, even when you are on the run. But first, it helps to understand my definition of "eating well." My simple definition is to:

1. Eat three kinds of food at each meal.
2. Eat two kinds of food at each snack.
3. Eat on a timeline—evenly throughout the day, and not in a crescendo, with the largest meal at the end of the day.
4. Choose to eat at least 80% to 90% of the calories from quality foods and, if desired, the remaining 10% to 20% from sweets and treats.

Because many of today's marathoners prefer to spend time training rather than cooking, take note: You don't have to be a good cook to eat well. You can still manage to eat well even if you are eating on the go.

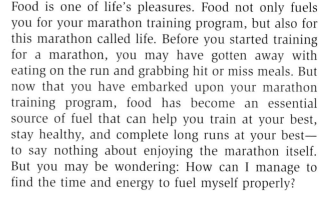

Some Top Sports Foods

The following top sports foods offer mainly cook-free and convenient best bets for people who eat and run.

Some of the best fruits for vitamins A and/or C:
oranges, grapefruit, tangerines, bananas, cantaloupe, strawberries, kiwi

Some of the best vegetables for vitamins A and/or C:
broccoli, spinach, green and red peppers, tomatoes, carrots, sweet potato, winter squash

Easy sources of calcium for strong bones:
Low-fat milk, yogurt, cheese, calcium-fortified orange juice, soy milk, and tofu

Convenient proteins for building and protecting muscles:
Deli roast beef, ham, turkey, canned tuna and salmon, hummus, peanut butter, tofu, cottage cheese

Grains for carbohydrates and fiber:
High-fiber breakfast cereals (preferably iron-enriched), wholesome breads and bagels, whole-grain crackers

Dietary Recommendations for Good Health

By following these dietary recommendations, you can substantially reduce your risk of developing heart disease and other diseases of aging.

- Balance calorie intake and physical activity to achieve and maintain a healthy body weight.
- Consume a diet rich in vegetables and fruits.
- Choose whole-grain, high-fiber foods.
- Consume fish, especially oily fish, at least twice a week.
- Limit your intake of saturated fat to <7% of energy, trans fat to <1% of energy, and cholesterol to <300 mg per day by
  —choosing lean meats and vegetable alternatives.
  —selecting fat-free (skim), 1%-fat, and low-fat dairy products.
  —minimizing intake of partially hydrogenated fats.
- Minimize your intake of beverages and foods with added sugars.
- Choose and prepare foods with little or no salt.
- If you consume alcohol, do so in moderation.
- When you eat food that is prepared outside of the home, follow these dietary recommendations.

Source: Diet and Lifestyle Recommendation Revision 2006: A Scientific Statement From the American Heart Association Nutrition Committee. A. Lichtenstein et al. Circulation 2006; 114:82-96.

To help guide optimal food choices, many countries and health organizations have created dietary guidelines. In 2005, the United States updated their guidelines to describe a healthy diet as one that emphasizes fruits, vegetables, whole grains, and fat-free or low-fat milk and dairy products; includes lean meats, poultry, fish, beans, eggs, and nuts; and is low in saturated fats, trans fats, cholesterol, salt (sodium), and added sugars. More specifically, this is what you want to keep in mind as you make your daily food choices:

- Try to eat at least two cups of fruit and 2.5 cups of vegetables per day. (This is the reference for a 2,000-calorie intake; most marathoners need more calories than that and should wisely consume some of those extra calories from fruits and vegetables.)
- Choose a variety of colors of fruits and vegetables each day: red apples, green peppers, orange carrots, white potatoes.
- Enjoy whole-grain products at least two times per day, such as oatmeal for breakfast and whole wheat bread for lunch. The rest of the recommended grains can come from enriched grain products, such as enriched pasta. In general, at least half the grains should come from whole grains. (Whole grains include whole wheat, brown rice, oats, corn, barley.)
- Drink 24 ounces (3 cups; 720 ml) per day of fat-free or low-fat milk or yogurt, or the calcium-equivalent in lowfat cheese (8 ounces of milk or yogurt = 240 ml = 1 cup = .75 ounces (20 g) of cheese).

- When selecting and preparing meat, poultry, dry beans, and milk or dairy products, make choices that are lean, low-fat, or fat-free.
- Limit your intake of saturated and trans fats and choose healthier oils such as olive and canola oils, nuts and nut butters, and oily fish such as salmon.

The trick to balancing the recommended servings of foods during your day is to plan to have at least three out of five food groups per meal, and one or two food groups per snack.

	Breakfast	Lunch	Snack	Dinner	Snack
Grain	oatmeal	bread		spaghetti	popcorn
Fruit	raisins	orange	apple		juice
Vegetable		baby carrots		tomato sauce	
Dairy	milk	yogurt	cheese	parmesan cheese	
Protein	almonds	peanut butter		ground turkey	

Carbohydrates for Your Sports Diet

By eating grains, fruits and vegetables as the foundation of each meal, you'll consume about 55 to 65 percent of your calories from carbohydrates. This is exactly what you need for a high-energy sports diet. These carbohydrates are stored in muscles in the form of glycogen, the energy you need to train hard day after day and to compete well on race day.

Grain foods are a popular source of carbohydrates for most active people. But some marathoners believe they will get fat if they eat breads, cereals and pastas at each meal. False. Carbohydrates are not fattening; excess calories are fattening (see Chapter 15: Weight Reduction for Marathoners). Your body needs carbs to fuel your muscles. Fruits and vegetables are also great sources of carbohydrates. But eating the recommended two cups (500 g) of fruits and 2.5 cups (600 gm) of vegetables is another story. As one marathoner sheepishly remarked, "I'm lucky if I eat that much in a week." The trick is to eat large portions. Most marathoners can easily enjoy a banana (1 cup fruit, 250 g) and 8 ounces (one cup, 240 ml) of orange juice in the morning. That's the minimal fruit duty for the day! A big bowl of salad filled with colorful tomatoes, carrots, and peppers can account for the minimal recommended 2.5 cups of vegetables.

If your goal is to be a strong runner in your golden years, today you want to start choosing meals abundant with fruits, vegetables and whole grain foods.

Fruits: Recommended Daily Intake—2 to 3 cups (500 to 700 g)

Orange Juice	8 ounces	240 ml
Apple	1 small	100 g
Banana	1 small	100 g
Caned Fruit	1 cup	240 g
Dried fruit	1/2 cup	80 g

Vegetables: Recommended Daily Intake—2.5 to 3 + cups (600 to 700 + g)

Broccoli	1 medium stalk	200 g
Spinach	2 cups, raw	60 g
Salad	1 average bowl	100 g
Spaghetti Sauce	1 cup	250 g

Fruits and vegetables are truly nature's vitamin pills, chock full of vitamin C (to help with healing), beta-carotene (to protect against cancer), fiber (to aid with regular bowel movements), and numerous other vitamins and minerals. The sidebar Eat More Veggies! (page 14) offers suggestions for ways to boost your veggie intake simply.

Protein for Your Sports Diet

Like carbohydrates, protein-rich foods are also an important part of your sports diet. You should eat a protein-rich food at each meal. Marathoners tend to either over- or underconsume protein, depending on their health consciousness and lifestyle. Whereas some marathoners frequently choose cheese omlets, fast food burgers and other meals filled with saturated fats, other marathoners bypass these foods in their efforts to eat a low-fat or vegetarain diet—but they neglect to replace beef with beans. For additional information and guidelines, see Chapter 6: Protein for Marathoners.

I've found that keeping a cooler packed with wholesome foods allows me to graze often and eat the items that fit my dietary requirements. To simplify the process of getting my trough ready, I choose pre-cut fruits and vegetables, dried fruits, nuts, energy bars, yogurt, etc. If I had to work hard at preparing these foods, this plan would quickly fall off my priority list.

John Correia, San Diego, CA

Recommended daily protein intake: *5 to 7 ounces*
                    (or ounce-equivalents; 140 to 200 g)

Protein-rich Foods	**Marathoner's Portion**	
	Number of ounces or ounce-equivalents	
Tuna	6 oz (170 g) can drained	3-4 ounce equivalents
Chicken	6 oz breast	6
Peanut Butter	2-4 tablespoons	1-2
Kidney Beans	1 cup	4

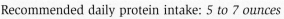

Eat More Veggies!

If you struggle to consume the recommended two to three servings of vegetables per day, the following tips may help you enhance your vegetable intake and your health.

- Eat more of the best vegetables, less of the rest. In general, dark green, deep yellow, orange, and red vegetables have far more nutrients than pale ones. Hence, if you dislike pale zucchini, summer squash, and cucumbers, don't work hard to acquire a taste for them. Instead, put your efforts into having more broccoli, spinach, and winter squash—the richly colored, more nutrient-dense choices.

- Eat colorful salads filled with tomatoes, green peppers, carrots, spinach, and dark lettuces. Pale salads with white lettuce, cucumbers, onions, celery, and other pale veggies offer little more than crunch. When smothered with dressing, this crunch becomes highly caloric. Alternatives to a pale restaurant salad include tomato juice, vegetable soup, a steamed veggie or, when you get home, a handful of raw baby carrots for an evening snack.

- Fortify spaghetti sauce with a box of frozen chopped broccoli or green peppers. Cook the veggies alongside the spaghetti (in a steamer over the pasta water) before you add it to the tomato sauce.

To meet your protein requirement for the day, you should consume not only one or two protein-rich foods per day but also the recommended two to three servings of calcium-rich dairy foods such as milk, yogurt and cheese (or other calcium-rich foods, such as calcium-fortified soy milk). Calcium is particularly important for growing teens and women who want to optimize bone density. For only 300 calories, even weight-conscious marathoners can easily contribute towards their protein intake plus achieve the recommended calcium intake by consuming:

- 8 oz. (240 ml) of milk or soy milk on breakfast cereal
- an 8 oz. (240 ml) cup of yogurt with lunch
- a (decaf) latte made with low-fat milk for an afternoon energizer

When choosing the recommended two to three daily servings of dairy foods, note that fat-free and low-fat products are preferable for heart health and calorie control, but you need not suffer with skim milk if you really don't like it. You can always cut back on fat in other parts of your diet. For example, Margie, a first-time marathoner, opted for cereal with reduced-fat (2%) milk (five grams of fat per cup), but saved on fat elsewhere in her diet by using fat-free salad dressing and low-fat granola. (For more information on dietary fat, see Chapter 7.)

Runners who prefer a dairy-free diet or are lactose intolerant should take special care to eat adequate amounts of nondairy calcium sources. See the sidebar, Calcium Equivalents (page 16), for food suggestions.

- Choose fast foods with the most veggies:
  - pizza with peppers, mushrooms, and extra tomato sauce
  - Chinese entrées stir-fried with vegetables
  - lunchtime V-8 juice instead of diet soda

- Even over-cooked vegetables are better than no vegetables. If your only option is over-cooked veggies from the cafeteria, eat them. While cooking does destroy some of the vegetable's nutrients, it does not destroy all of them. Any vegetable is better than no vegetable!

- Keep frozen vegetables stocked in your freezer, ready and waiting. They are quick and easy to prepare, won't spoil quickly, and have more nutrients than "fresh" vegetables that have been in the store and your refrigerator for a few days. Because cooking (more than freezing) reduces a vegetable's nutritional content:
  - quickly cook vegetables only until tender crisp and use the cooking water as a broth
  - microwave vegetables in a covered dish
  - stir-fry them with very little olive oil

- When all else fails, eat fruit to help compensate for lack of vegetables. The best alternatives include bananas, oranges, grapefruit, melon, strawberries, and kiwi. These choices are rich in many of the same nutrients found in vegetables.

Sweets and Treats

Although nutritionists recommend eating a wholesome diet based on grains, fruits, and vegetables, some marathoners eat far too many sweets and treats. If you have a junk-food diet, you may be able correct this imbalance by eating more wholesome foods before you get too hungry. Marathoners who get too hungry tend to choose sugary, fatty foods (such as apple pie, instead of apples). A simple solution to the junk-food diet is to prevent hunger by eating wholesome meals.

Take note: you need not eat a "perfect diet" (no fats, no sugar) to have a good diet. Nothing is nutritionally wrong with having a cookie for dessert after having eaten a sandwich, milk, and fruit for lunch. But much is wrong with eating cookies for lunch and skipping the sandwich. That's when nutrition and performance problems arise.

The key to balancing fats and sugars appropriately in your diet is to abide the following guidelines:

- 10 percent of your calories can appropriately come from refined sugar (about 200–300 calories from sugar per day for most marathoners)
- 25 percent of your calories can appropriately come from fat (about 450–750 calories from fat per day, or roughly 50–85 grams of fat per day)

Hence, moderate amounts of chips, cookies, and ice cream can fit into an overall healthful food plan.

Calcium Equivalents

The recommended daily calcium intake is:

Age Group	Calcium (mg)
Teens, 9-18 years	1,300
Adults, 19-50 years	1,000
Adults, 51+ years	1,200

Source: Dietary Reference Intakes, National Academy of Science, 1997

The following foods all provide about 300 milligrams of calcium. Two to three choices per day, or one at each meal, will contribute to meeting your calcium needs.

Calcium-rich Dairy Foods	Amount
Milk, whole or skim	1 cup (240 ml)
Yogurt	1 cup (230 g)
Cheese	1 1/2 ounces (45 g)
Cottage cheese	2 cups (450 g)
Frozen yogurt	1 1/2 cups (150 g)

Proteins	
Soy milk	1 cup (240 ml)
Tofu	8 oz. (1/2 cake; 250 g)
Salmon, canned with bones	5 ounces (140 g)
Sardines, canned with bones	3 ounces (85 g)
Almonds	4 ounces (110 g)

Vegetables	
Broccoli, cooked	3 cups (550 g)
Collard or turnip greens, cooked	1 cup (150 g)
Kale or mustard greens, cooked	1 1/2 cups (220 g)

Need Some Help Shaping Up Your Diet?

If you want personalized dietary advice, I recommend that you seek professional advice from a registered dietitian (RD) who specializes in sports nutrition and, ideally, is board certified as a specialist in sports Dietetics (CSSD). To find a sports nutritionist in your area, use the referral networks at the American Dietetic Association's website (www.eatright.org) or the website of the ADA's practice group of sports dietitians (www.SCANdpg.org). Or try checking a search engine for "sports nutritionist, your city." You'll be glad you did! This personal nutrition coach can help you more easily win with good nutrition.

Recipes for Success: Vegetables 101: Basic Cooking Tips

Vegetables are nutrient-rich, but cooking can destroy some of their nutritional value. To get the most nutrients from your vegetables, handle them properly so they have minimal exposure to air, heat, water, and light—the four elements that reduce their nutritional value.

- To reduce exposuse to air: Store fresh vegetables in plastic containers. Cook covered.
- To reduce exposure to heat: Store fresh vegetables in the refrigerator; minimize cooking time to enhance the flavor and nutritional value.
- To reduce exposure to water: Cook in minimal water, stir-fry, or microwave.
- To reduce exposure to light: Store in a dark place (inside the fridge!); cook in a covered pan.

Basic Steamed Vegetables
1. Wash vegetables thoroughly; prepare and cut into pieces keeping the skin or peel, if appropriate.
2. Put 1/2 inch (1 cm) water in the bottom of a pan that has a tight cover.
3. Bring the water to a boil. Add the vegetables. Or put the vegetables in a steamer basket and put this in the saucepan with 1 inch (2 cm) of water.
4. Cover the pan tightly and cook over medium heat until the vegetables are tender yet crisp (about 3 minutes for spinach, 10 minutes for broccoli, 15 minutes for sliced carrots).
5. Drain the vegetables, reserving the cooking water for soup or sauces, or simply drink it as a broth.

If you wish to add some seasonings before or after cooking, here are some nice combinations:

Basil	Green beans, tomatoes, zucchini
Oregano	Zucchini, mushrooms, tomatoes, onions
Dill	Green beans, carrots, peas, potatoes
Cinnamon	Spinach, winter squash, sweet potatoes
Marjoram	Celery, greens
Nutmeg	Corn, cauliflower, green beans
Thyme	Artichokes, mushrooms, peas, carrots
Parsley	Sprinkled on any vegetable

Basic Microwaved Vegetables
Microwave cookery is perfect for vegetables because microwaves cook the veggies quickly and without water, thereby retaining a greater percentage of the nutrients than with conventional methods.

1. Wash the vegetables and cut them into bite-size pieces. Put them in a microwavable container with a cover.

2. Microwave until tender yet crisp; stir half-way through cooking, so they cook evenly. The amount of time will vary according to your particular microwave oven and the amount of vegetable you are cooking. Start off with three minutes for a single serving; larger servings take longer. The vegetables will continue cooking after you remove them from the oven, so plan that into your cooking time.

Basic Stir-fried Vegetables

Vegetables stir-fried until tender and crisp are very flavorful, colorful, and nutritious, but they do have more calories than if steamed. If weight is an issue, be sure to add only a minimal amount of oil (olive, canola, sesame) to the cooking pan.

Some popular stir-fry combinations include:
- Carrots, broccoli, and mushrooms
- Onions, green peppers, zucchini, and tomatoes
- Chinese cabbage, bok choy, and water chestnuts

1. Wash, drain well (to prevent the water from spattering when the vegetables are added), and cut the vegetables of your choice into bite-sized pieces or 1/8-inch slices. Whenever possible, slice vegetables diagonally to increase the surface area; this allows for faster cooking. Try to make the pieces uniform so they will cook evenly.

2. Heat the skillet over high heat. Add 1 to 3 teaspoons of oil, just enough to coat the bottom of the pan. Optional: Add a slice of ginger root or some minced garlic, stir-frying for one minute to add flavor.

3. Add the vegetables that take longest to cook (carrots, cauliflower, broccoli); a few minutes later add the remaining ones (mushrooms, bean sprouts, cabbage, spinach). Constantly lift and turn the vegetables to coat them with oil.

4. Add a little bit of water (1/4 to 1/2 cup), then cover and steam the vegetables for 2 to 5 minutes. Adjust the heat to prevent scorching.

5. Don't overcrowd the pan. Cook small batches at a time.

6. Optional add-ins: soy sauce, beef, chicken, tofu, rice, or noodles.

7. To thicken the juices, stir in a mixture of 2 teaspoons cornstarch diluted into 1 tablespoon water. Add more water or broth if this makes the sauce too thick.

RECIPE

Optional: Garnish with toasted sesame seeds, mandarin orange sections, or pineapple chunks.

Basic Baked Vegetables

If you are baking chicken, potatoes, or a casserole, you might as well make good use of the oven and bake the vegetables too. Some popular suggestions include:
- Eggplant halves sprinkled with garlic powder
- Zucchini with onions and oregano
- Carrots with ginger
- Sliced sweet potato with apple

1. Put the vegetables (seasoned as desired) in a covered baking dish with a small amount of water, or wrap them in foil.
2. Bake at 350 degrees for 20 to 30 minutes (depending on the size of the chunks) until tender and crisp. Caution: With foil-wrapped vegetables, be careful when opening the foil. The escaping steam might burn you.

Adapted from: *Nancy Clark's Sports Nutrition Guidebook, Third Edition* (Human Kinetics, 2003).

Chapter 2

Breakfast:
The Meal of
Champions

You've undoubtedly heard this from your mother. And now you'll hear it from me. Breakfast is the most important meal of the day! Yes, there is a hurdle to eating breakfast—you have to find the time to do so—but the benefits far outweigh the costs. Breakfast eaters tend to:

- eat a more nutritious, lower fat diet (a wholesome breakfast can reduce the urge for junk food at night)
- have lower blood cholesterol levels
- enjoy success with weight control. (In one survey, 88% of dieters who lost weight and kept it off became religious breakfast eaters; only 4% rarely ate breakfast.) (Wyatt, 2002)
- are mentally alert and more productive (just like school kids who eat breakfast)
- have more energy to enjoy exercise either in the morning or later that day

As an athlete, you should eat even-sized meals about every four hours, starting with breakfast within three hours of waking. From petite female runners on a 2,000 calorie per day weight reduction diet, to tall men who devour 3,600 calories per day, marathoners deserve to eat a hefty 500 to 900 calories for their morning meal(s), including a pre- and post-morning-run snack followed by breakfast at the office. (See Chapter 14 for information on how to calculate your calorie needs for breakfast and the entire day.) By spending one-fourth of your calories in the morning, you will have adequate energy to start your busy day, to say nothing of abating hunger and the 10:00 a.m. visit from the cookie monster.

> **Breakfast is not my favorite meal of the day, but I soon learned it was essential to my overall endurance. My training sessions and times were markedly worse when I skipped breakfast. A bagel or cereal in the morning works wonders for me!**
>
> *Shelley Smith, CO*

Despite my clear message about breakfast being the most important meal of the day, I have to coax my clients to experiment with eating (more) breakfast. Far too many marathoners under-eat in the morning. Some fear if they eat more at breakfast, they'll get fat. Or if they eat breakfast, they'll feel more hunger than if they abstain. Let's take at look at some standard breakfast excuses—and solutions.

I don't have time: Lack of priority is the real problem, not lack of time. If you can make time to train, you can make time to fuel for your training. Even if you choose to sleep to the last minute before dragging yourself out of bed, you can still choose to eat breakfast on the way to work. Breakfast need not be an elaborate occasion. You can quickly prepare a simple breakfast to eat on the run:

- a baggie filled with raisins, almonds, and granola
- a tortilla rolled with a slice or two of low-fat cheese
- a peanut butter and honey sandwich on wholesome bread
- a glass of milk, then a banana while walking to the bus or train

- a travel mug filled with a fruit smoothie or protein shake (there will always be coffee at the office)
- an energy bar and a banana during the morning commute

The key to breakfast on the run is to plan ahead. Prepare your breakfast the night before so that you can simply grab it and go during the morning rush. For example, on the weekends, you might want to make banana bread (see my favorite recipe at the end of this chapter) or buy a dozen bagels. Pre-slice the bread or the bagels, wrap the desired portion in individual plastic bags, and put them in the freezer. Take one out of the freezer at night so breakfast will be ready and waiting in the morning.

Breakfast interferes with my training schedule: If you are an early morning runner or walker (5:00–7:00 a.m.), you will likely exercise better and avoid an energy crash if you eat part of your breakfast before you exercise (assuming your stomach can tolerate food, of course). Coffee with extra milk, a swig of juice, a chunk of bagel, or piece of bread are popular choices that can get your blood sugar on the upswing, contribute to greater stamina, and help you feel more awake. If you prefer to abstain, at least have a hefty bedtime snack the night before. (Chapter 9: Fueling Before You Exercise explains in greater detail the importance of morning food.)

Breakfast is equally important if you exercise at mid-day or in the afternoon. You need to fuel up in order to do a quality workout that afternoon. Breakfast is essential if you are doing double workouts. Because your muscles are hungriest for carbohydrates within the first hour after hard exercise, a quick and easy recovery breakfast will set the stage for a strong second workout.

> **During training, we encourage our marathoners to start eating breakfast— even if they aren't breakfast people—to help prevent "the bonk." When someone bonks, we quiz them about what they ate that day. Inevitably, they have skipped breakfast. They learn never to do that again!**
>
> *Matt Keil, San Jose, CA*

I sometimes hear marathoners express the concern that eating breakfast interferes with their upcoming workout; that the food will sit heavily in the stomach or "talk back." This is unlikely. A low-fat meal at 7:00 to 8:00 a.m. (such as cereal and low-fat milk) should be well digested by noon. Try it; you'll probably see a positive difference in your energy level.

I'm not hungry in the morning: If you have no morning appetite, the chances are you ate your breakfast calories the night before. Huge dinner? Ice cream? Too many cookies before bedtime? The solution to having no morning appetite is, obviously, to eat less at night so that you can start the day off hungry.

If running first thing in the morning "kills your appetite" (due to the rise in body temperature), keep in mind that you will be hungry within a few hours when you have cooled down. Plan ahead, so when the hunger horrors hit, you will have healthful brunch options ready and waiting. Otherwise, you'll be likely to grab whatever's easy, which may include doughnuts, pastries, cookies, and other high-fat foods.

I'm on a diet: Too many weight-conscious people start their diet at breakfast. Bad idea. Breakfast skippers tend to gain weight and to be heavier than breakfast eaters. A satisfying breakfast prevents you from getting too hungry and overeating.

Your best bet for successful dieting is to eat during the day, burn off the calories, and then eat a lighter meal at night. Chapter 15 has more details about how to lose weight and have energy to train.

> I still find it hard to believe that when I started eating more at breakfast and lunch, I lost weight. I felt as though I was cheating all the time. My running times even improved because I was actually well-fueled instead of half-starved.
>
> *Laura Perkins,*
> *New York City, NY*

Breakfast makes me hungrier: Many marathoners complain that if they eat breakfast, they seem to get hungrier and eat more all day. This may result from thinking they have already "blown their diets" by eating breakfast, so they might as well keep overeating, then start dieting again the next day. Wrong.

Successful diets start at breakfast. If you feel hungry after breakfast you probably ate too little breakfast. For example, 100 calories of toast with jam is enough to whet your appetite but not to satisfy your calorie needs. Try budgeting about one-quarter of your calories for breakfast— 500–600 calories for most 120–150-pound runners. This translates into two slices of toast with jam, a banana, low-fat yogurt, and juice; or yogurt and a bagel with peanut butter.

Note: If you overeat at breakfast, you can easily resolve the problem by eating less at lunch or dinner. You won't be as physically hungry for those meals and will be able to easily eat smaller portions.

The Breakfast of Champions

By now, I hope I've convinced you that breakfast is indeed the most important meal of the day for marathoners. What should you eat, you wonder? If you feel like cooking, enjoy hot oatmeal, French toast, or pancakes.

But if you are looking for a cook-free choice, I highly recommend cereal. Cereal is quick, convenient, and filled with the calcium, iron, carbohydrates, fiber, and other nutrients active people need. A bowl of bran cereal with fruit and low-fat milk provides a well-balanced meal that includes three of the five food groups (grain, milk, and fruit) and sets the stage for an overall low-fat diet.

Cereal is versatile. You can eat it dry if you're on the run, or preferably with low-fat milk and/or yogurt for a calcium booster. You can mix brands and vary the flavor with different toppings:

- sliced banana
- blueberries (a handful of frozen ones taste great—especially if microwaved)
- raisins
- canned fruit
- cinnamon
- maple syrup
- vanilla yogurt

My personal favorite is to put a mix of cereals in my bowl, top it with fruit, heat it in the microwave oven for 30 to 60 seconds, and then add cold milk. It's like eating fruit cobbler!

How to Choose the Best Breakfast Cereal

Needless to say, all cereals are not created equal. Some offer more nutritional value than others. Here are four tips to help you make the best choices.

1. *Choose iron-enriched cereals with at least 25 percent of the Daily Value for iron to help prevent anemia.*

Note, however, the iron in breakfast cereals is poorly absorbed compared to the iron in lean red meats. But you can enhance iron absorption by drinking a glass of orange juice or enjoying another source of vitamin C (such as grapefruit, cantaloupe, strawberries, or kiwi) along with the cereal. Any iron is better than no iron.

If you tend to eat "all-natural" types of cereals, such as granola and shredded wheat, be aware that these types have "no additives," hence no added iron. You might want to mix and match all-natural brands with iron-enriched brands (or make the effort to eat iron-rich foods at other meals).

2. *Choose fiber-rich bran cereals with more than 5 grams of fiber per serving.*

Fiber not only helps prevent constipation but also is a protective nutrient that may reduce your risk of colon cancer and heart disease. Bran cereals are the best sources of fiber, more so than even fruits and vegetables. Choose from All-Bran, 40% Bran Flakes, Raisin Bran, Bran

Nontraditional Breakfasts

Not everyone likes cereal for breakfast, nor do they want to cook eggs or pancakes. If you are stumped by what to eat for breakfast, choose a food that you enjoy. After all, you'll be more likely to eat breakfast if it tastes good. Remember that any food—even a cookie (preferably oatmeal raisin, rather than chocolate chip)—is better than nothing.
How about:
- **leftover pizza**
- **leftover Chinese food**
- **mug of tomato soup**
- **potato zapped in the microwave while you take your shower**
- **tuna sandwich**
- **peanut butter and apple**
- **protein bar**

Breakfast is particularly important for people who walk or run in the morning. Don't try to exercise on an empty stomach; you'll lag on energy

Chex, Fiber One or any of the numerous cereals with "bran" or "fiber" in the name. You can also mix high- and low-fiber cereals (Rice Crispies + Fiber One; Special K + Raisin Bran) to boost their fiber value.

Note: If you have trouble with diarrhea when running, you may want to forgo bran cereals. The extra fiber may aggravate the situation.

3. *Choose cereals with whole grains listed among the first ingredients.*
Whole grains include whole wheat, brown rice, corn, and oats; these should be listed first in the ingredients. In my opinion, you should pay more attention to a cereal's grain content than its sugar or sodium (salt) content. Here's why:
- Sodium is a concern primarily for people with high blood pressure. Most runners have low blood pressure and are unlikley to suffer health consequences from choosing cereals with a little added salt.
- Sugar is simply a carbohydrate that fuels your muscles. Yes, sugar calories are nutritionally empty calories. But when they are combined with milk, banana, and the cereal itself, the twenty empty calories in five grams of added sugar are insignificant. Obviously, sugar-filled frosted flakes and kids' cereals with fifteen grams of sugar or more per serving are somewhat more like dessert than breakfast. Hence, try to limit your breakfast choices to cereals with fewer than five grams of added sugar per serving. Eat the sugary ones for snacks or dessert, if desired, or mix a little with low-sugar cereals.

4. *Choose primarily low-fat cereals with less than two grams of fat per serving.*
High-fat cereals, such as some brands of granola and crunchy cookie-type cereals can add unexpected fat and calories to your sports diet. Select low-fat brands for the foundation of your breakfast, then use only a sprinkling of the higher-fat treats, if desired, for a topping.

Mix 'n Match Cereals
When it comes to cereals, you may not find one that meets all of your standards for high fiber, high iron and low fat, but you can always mix-and-match to create a winning combination.

Brand	Iron (%DV)	Fiber (g)	Fat (g)
"Ideal cereal"	> 25%	> 5	< 2
Cheerios, 1 cup (30g)	45%	3	2
Wheaties, 1 cup (30 g)	45%	3	1
Kashi Go Lean, 1 cup (52 g)	10%	10	1
Raisin Bran, Kellogg's. 1 cup (59 g)	25%	7	1.5
Fiber One, 1/2 cup (30 g)	25%	14	1
Quaker 100% Natural, 1/2 cup (48 g)	6%	3	6
Oat Squares, Quaker, 1 cup (60 g)	80%	4	2.5
Cap'n Crunch, 3/4 cup (30 g)	25%	1	1.5

Summary

What you eat in the morning provides fuel for a high energy day and stronger workouts. Breakfast helps novice and experienced marathoners alike to make their way to the winners' circle! Even dieters can enjoy breakfast without the fear of "getting fat"—that is, breakfast helps curb evening appetite so that dieters can eat lighter at night.

If you generally skip breakfast, at least give breakfast a try during your marathon training. You'll soon learn why breakfast is the meal of champions!

Recipe for Success: Banana Bread

When you are confronted with bananas that are getting too ripe, consider making this recipe for banana bread. You'll enjoy it for a quick but hearty breakfast, lunch, or snack. Add some peanut butter and a glass of low-fat milk for a well-balanced meal and energy for the long run.

3 large bananas, the riper the better
1 egg or 2 egg whites
2 tbsp. (30 g) oil, preferably canola
1/3 to 1/2 cup (70-100 g) sugar
1/4 cup (60 ml) milk
1 tsp. (5 g) salt, as desired
1 tsp. (5 g) baking soda
1/2 tsp. (2.3) baking powder
1 1/2 cups (180 g) flour, preferably half white, half whole-wheat

Preheat oven to 350°F (175°C).
Spray a 9x5-inch loaf pan with cooking spray.
In a large bowl, mash the bananas with a fork.
Add the egg, oil, sugar, milk, and salt. Beat well, then add the baking soda and baking powder.
Gently blend the flour into the banana mixture. Stir for 20 seconds or until just moistened.
Pour the batter into the prepared pan.
Bake at 350°F for 45 minutes or until a toothpick inserted near the middle comes out clean.

YIELD: 1 loaf, 12 slices
Total calories: 1,600
Calories per slice: 140

	Grams
Carbohydrates	24
Protein	3
Fat	3

From: *Nancy Clark's Sport Nutrition Guidebook, Third Edition* (Human Kinetics, 2003)

Chapter 3

How to Manage Lunch, Snacks, and Dinner

Whereas breakfast is the most important meal of your training diet, lunch is the second most important. In fact, I encourage marathoners to eat TWO lunches! One lunch at 11:00 a.m., when you first start to get hungry, then a second lunch at 3:00 to 4:00 in the afternoon, when the munchies strike. If you train in the morning, these lunches refuel your muscles. If you train in the late afternoon, these lunches prepare you for a strong workout. And in either case, two lunches curb your appetite so you are not starving at the end of the day and have the energy to cook a nutritious dinner.

I invite you to experiment with this two-lunch concept. If you are like most of my clients, you'll find yourself looking forward to a second sandwich to boost your energy at the end of the day. Afraid that two lunches will be fattening? Fear not; a second lunch does not mean additional calories. You'll simply be trading your afternoon cookies and evening ice cream for a wholesome afternoon meal. No longer will you search for evening snacks; you ate them earlier.

What's for Lunch?

Marathoners commonly have three options for lunch: pack your own, pick up some fast-food, or enjoy a hot meal from the cafeteria at work or school. You can eat healthfully in each of these scenarios; just remember to enjoy three kinds of wholesome food with each meal (bread + peanut butter + banana; pizza crust + tomato sauce + cheese; chicken + rice + vegetables) and at least 500 to 600 calories per meal (based on a 2,000- to 2,400-calorie food plan, the amount appropriate for marathoners who want to lose weight; non-dieters can target about 600 to 800 calories per meal).

Eating a hot meal in the middle of the day can make the evening easier for marathoners who train in the late afternoon, arrive home starved and don't feel like cooking. Enjoying a nice meal at noon can make a soup-and-sandwich dinner more acceptable. For hot meal suggestions, see the section on page 34 on Dinner and Marathoners.

Pack Your Own Lunches

Packing your own lunch is a good way to save money, time, and oftentimes saturated fat and calories if you are organized enough to have the right foods on hand. Good nutrition certainly starts in the supermarket! One trick to packing your lunch is to schedule "food shopping" into your training log. A second trick is to make lunch the night before.

The following suggestions may help you pack a super sports lunch.
- To prevent sandwich bread from getting stale, keep in it the freezer and take out the slices as needed. Bread thaws in minutes at room temperature, or in seconds in the microwave oven.
- Make several sandwiches at one time, then store them in the freezer. The frozen sandwich will be thawed—and fresh—by lunch time. Sliced turkey, lean roast beef, peanut butter, and leftover pizza freeze nicely. Don't freeze eggs, mayonnaise, jelly, lettuce, tomatoes, or raw veggies.

- Instead of eating a dry sandwich with no mayonnaise, add moistness using low-fat mayonnaise; low-fat bottled salad dressings, such as ranch or creamy Italian; mustard or ketchup; lettuce and tomato.
- Return to eating peanut butter; it is filled with health-protective fat that reduces your risk of heart disease and diabetes. Enjoy peanut butter (or other nut butters) with sliced banana, raisins, dates, sunflower seeds, apple slices, and/or celery slices.
- Add zip to a (low-fat) cheese sandwich with oregano, Italian seasonings, green peppers, and/or tomatoes.
- Pack leftover soups, chili, and pasta dinners for the next day's lunch. You can either eat the leftovers cold or heat them in the office microwave oven.

Fast-Food Lunches

Because of busy schedules, few marathoners make the effort to organize their lunch plans in advance. Hence, fast foods can save the day—or they can spoil your sports diet. The good news is most quick-service restaurants now offer more low-fat foods than ever before. But, you'll still be confronted by the fatty temptations that jump out at you. Before succumbing to grease, remind yourself that you will feel better and feel better about yourself if you eat well.

Here are suggestions for some lower-fat choices:

Dunkin' Donuts:	Low-fat muffin, bagel, juice, bean or broth-based soups, hot cocoa
Deli:	Bagel with bean or broth-based soups; sandwiches or subs with lots of bread and half the filling, little or no mayonnaise (or, ask for two extra slices of bread or a second roll to make a sandwich for your second lunch with the excessive meat.)
McDonald's:	Grilled chicken sandwich with high-carb fluids, such as juices, milkshakes, and yes, even soft drinks (in moderation) can fuel your muscles
Wendy's:	Bowl of chili with a plain baked potato
Taco Bell:	Bean burrito
Pizza:	Thick-crust with extra veggies rather than extra cheese or pepperoni
Pasta:	Spaghetti or ziti with tomato sauce and a glass of low-fat milk for protein. Be cautious of lasagna, tortellini, or manicotti that are filled with cheese (i.e., are high in saturated fat).
Chinese:	Hot and sour or wonton soup; plain rice with stir-fried entrées such as beef and broccoli or chicken with pea pods. Request the food be cooked with minimal oil. Limit fried appetizers and fried entrées.

Salad for Lunch

Salads, whether served as a main dish or an accompaniment, are a simple way to boost your intake of fresh vegetables; that's good! But as a marathoner, you need a substantial, carbohydrate-based lunch; most salads get the bulk of their calories from salad oil; bad! You'll be better able to fuel your muscles if you choose a sandwich with a side salad for lunch rather than eat just a big salad for the entire meal.

Three tricks to making a healthy sports salad are:
1. Choose a variety of colorful vegetables—dark green lettuces, red tomatoes, yellow peppers, orange carrots—for a variety of vitamins and minerals.

2. Monitor the dressing. Some marathoners drown 50 calories of healthful salad ingredients with 400 calories of blue cheese dressing!

3. Add extra carbohydrates:
- dense vegetables, such as corn, peas, beets, carrots
- beans and legumes, such as chick-peas, kidney beans, and three-bean salad
- cooked rice or pasta
- oranges, apples, raisins, grapes, craisins
- toasted croutons
- whole-grain bread or roll on the side

Salads

Here are how some popular salad ingredients compare. Note that the ones with the most color have the most nutritional value.

Salad Ingredient	Vitamin C (mg)	Vitamin A (IU)	Magnesium (mg)
Daily Value	60	5,000	400
Broccoli, 5" stalk (180 g)	110	2,500	24
Green pepper, 1/2 (70 g)	65	210	20
Spinach, 2 cups raw (110 g)	50	8,100	90
Tomato, medium (120 g)	25	760	15
Romaine, 2 cups (110 g)	30	3,000	10
Iceburg, 2 cups (110 g)	5	360	5
Cucumber, 1/2 medium (150 g)	10	325	15
Celery, 1 stalk (40 g)	5	55	4

If you choose to use regular dressings, try to select ones made with olive oil for both a nice flavor and health-protective fats. If you want to reduce your fat intake, simply dilute regular dressings with water, more vinegar, or even milk (for ranch and other mayonnaise-based dressings). Or, choose from the plethora of low-fat and fat-free salad dressings. Low-fat dressings are good not only for salads, but also sandwiches, baked potatoes, and dips.

If you know the vegetables you buy for salads tend to wilt in your refrigerator, consider frequent trips to the salad bar at the grocery store and deli as an alternative to tossing veggies that spoil before you find the chance to eat them.

Solving the Four O'Clock Munchies Problem

Many marathoners believe eating in the afternoon is sinful. They self-impose "Thou shalt not snack" as an Eleventh Commandment. Then, they succumb and feel guilty. As I have mentioned before, hunger is simply your body's request for fuel. Hunger is not bad nor wrong. It is a normal physiological function. You can expect to get hungry every 4 hours. For example, if you eat lunch at noon, you can appropriately be hungry by 4:00. Eat something—preferably a second lunch! "Second lunch" conjures up visions of real food—a second sandwich, a mug of soup, or peanut butter on crackers and a (decaf) latte. In comparison, "afternoon snack" suggests candy, cookies and sweets. Marathoners who fail to eat enough at breakfast and first lunch generally crave afternoon sweets. The preferred solution to sweet cravings is not to eat chocolate, but to prevent the cravings by eating more food earlier in the day.

A second lunch is particularly important for dieters. As I will discuss in Chapter 15, a planned afternoon lunch of 300 to 500 calories (or whatever fits into your calorie budget) will prevent extreme hunger and reduce the risk of blowing your diet.

Second Lunch Suggestions

Some marathoners enjoy a second sandwich for their second lunch. But others like to graze on two or three wholesome snacks from this list. If you carry snacks with you, or keep a supply of "emergency food" in your desk drawer that's ready and waiting for the 4 o'clock munchies, you can avoid the temptations that lurk in every convenience store, vending machine, or bakery. Try to pick items from two or three different food groups, such as carrots + cottage cheese + crackers; or graham crackers + peanut butter + apple.

Perishable snacks to carry with you or buy fresh:
- whole wheat bagel
- low-fat bran muffin
- microwaved potato
- yogurt, low-fat
- cottage cheese, low-fat
- cheese sticks, low-fat
- thick-crust pizza
- fresh fruit
- baby carrots
- leftover pasta
- frozen meal
- peanut butter sandwich

Nonperishable snacks to keep stocked in your desk drawer:
- cold cereal (by the handful right out of the box or in a bowl with milk)
- hot cereal (packets of instant oatmeal are easy)
- reduced-fat microwave popcorn
- canned soup
- canned tuna
- low-fat crackers (Ak-Mak, Wasa, Melba Toast)
- graham crackers
- low-fat granola bars
- energy bars
- juice boxes or bottles
- dried fruit
- peanut butter
- nuts, trail mix

Vending machine snacks: Vending-machine cuisine offers tough choices. But tucked between the lackluster choices, you may be able to find pretzels, peanuts, juice, yogurt, or even an apple. The good part about vending-machine snacks is that they are limited in size (e.g., only three cookies instead of the whole bag) and generally provide only 200 to 400 calories, not 2,000.

If trying to decide between fatty or sugary choices (i.e., chips vs. jelly beans), remember that the sugar in jelly beans will appropriately fuel your muscles, whereas the fat in the chips will clog the arteries. (After eating a sugary snack, be sure to brush or rinse your teeth.)

Cookie Monster snacks: If it's cookies, brownies, an ice cream sundae, or any other such treat that you crave once a week or so, I recommend you satisfy your hankering by enjoying the treat in place of one of your lunches. Simply trade in your lunch calories for treat calories so you won't be overeating. You won't destroy your health with an occasional treat, as long as your overall diet tends to be wholesome. Looking at the weekly picture, you want to target a diet that averages 90% quality foods, 10% treats.

Dinner and Marathoners

Dinnertime generally marks the end of the work day, a time to relax and enjoy a pleasant meal, that is, if you have the energy to prepare it. The trick to dining on a balanced dinner—the protein-starch-vegetable kind that mom used to make with at least three kinds of foods—is to arrive home with enough energy to cook. This means fueling your body and brain with adequate calories prior to dinnertime—with a second lunch.

If you are far from being a master chef, you might want to take a cooking class at your local center for adult education. But no number of cooking classes will help if you arrive home too hungry to cook or make wise food choices.

Quick Fixes: Dinner Tips for Hungry Runners

Because good nutrition starts in the supermarket, you have a far better chance of achieving a super sports diet when your kitchen is well stocked with appropriate foods. You might want to muster up your energy to marathon shop at the discount or warehouse food store once every two or three weeks and really shop so that you have enough food to last for a while. To help accomplish this goal, post a copy of the *Marathoner's Basic Shopping List* (next page) on your refrigerator and check off the foods you need.

By keeping your kitchen well-stocked with basic foods, you will have the makings for simple meals such as:
- Spaghetti with tomato sauce plus hamburger, ground turkey, tofu, beans, cheese cottage, grated cheese, and/or vegetables
- English muffin or pita pizzas
- Tuna noodle casserole

Marathoner's Basic Shopping List

Keep this on your refrigerator and be sure to notice when an item gets low and needs to be replaced.

Cupboard: cereal, spaghetti, spaghetti sauce, (brown) rice, (whole grain) crackers, baked corn chips, kidney beans, baked beans, refried beans, tuna, peanut butter, soups (mushroom for making casseroles, lentil, minestrone, hearty bean), baking potatoes, V-8 or other vegetable juices.

Refrigerator: low-fat cheddar, mozzarella and cottage cheese, low-fat milk and yogurt, Parmesan cheese, eggs, tofu, tortillas, carrots, lettuce, tomatoes, oranges, bananas (when refrigerated, the banana peel turns black but the fruit itself is fine and lasts longer).

Freezer: whole-grain bagels, whole-wheat pita, English muffins, multigrain bread, orange juice concentrate, broccoli, spinach, winter squash, ground turkey, extra-lean hamburger, chicken (pieces frozen individually in baggies).

- Soup and sandwiches (tuna, toasted cheese, peanut butter with banana)
- Microwaved potato topped with cottage cheese, baked beans, or yogurt
- Peanut butter crackers and V-8 juice
- Bean burritos (frozen, or made with canned refried beans + salsa + tortilla)

Some runners use their morning shower/shave time to cook 1.5 cups of raw rice while getting ready for work. Come dinner time, they simply brown one pound of lean hamburger or ground turkey in a large skillet, dump in the cooked rice, and then add whatever is handy. By cooking 1 1/2 cups of raw rice for each pound of raw lean meat, they generate two generous sports meals with 60 percent of the calories from carbohydrates.

Some popular creations with rice and ground meat include:
- Mexican—canned beans + chili powder + grated low-fat cheddar cheese + diced tomatoes
- Chinese—broccoli zapped in the microwave oven while the meat cooks + soy sauce
- Italian—green beans + Italian seasonings, such as basil, oregano, and garlic powder
- American—grated low-fat cheddar cheese + onion browned with the meat + diced tomatoes

Quick and Easy Meal Ideas

Here are some ideas for quick and easy meals:

- pasta with clam sauce, tomato sauce, and/or frozen vegetables, and/or low-fat cheese
- canned beans, rinsed and then spooned over rice, pasta, or salads
- frozen dinners, supplemented with whole-grain bread and fresh fruit
- Pierogies, tortellini, and burritos from the frozen food section
- baked potato topped with cottage cheese
- whole-grain cereal (hot or cold) with fruit and low-fat milk
- thick-crust pizza, fresh or frozen, then reheated in the toaster oven
- bean soups, homemade, canned, or from the deli
- quick-cooking brown rice—made double for the next day's rice and bean salad
- stir-fry, using pre-cut vegetables from the market, salad bar, or freezer

Soup and Marathoners

Thick and hearty soups, abundant with carbs from rice, barley, or beans, are welcomed foods for marathoners who need not only the carbs to refuel muscles but also the broth to replace sweat losses. I like to keep soups and stews on hand for quick evening meals that simply need to be heated. What a wonderful greeting upon returning from a long winter run! A bowl of warm soup is a relatively effortless dinner, thanks to the microwave oven.

If you frequently make soups or stews, you might want to:

- Save the cooking water from vegetables in a jar in the refrigerator to use as a soup base.
- Limit the seasonings so that you can add the seasoning-of-the-day into the individual portion you will be eating. That way, you can have Chinese-style chicken soup one day, curried chicken soup another, and Mexican a third.

There is nothing wrong with using canned soups or broths for the foundation of a quick and easy meal. Because the canned products tend to have more sodium than do some homemade soups and stews, runners with high blood pressure should choose the low-sodium canned soups.

Here are some ways to convert plain ol' canned soup into a more exotic meal, light supper, or snack:

- **Combine soups**
  onion and chicken noodle
  tomato and vegetable

- **Add ingredients**
  diced celery, broccoli, tomatoes, or whatever fresh or frozen vegetable is handy
  leftover rice, noodles, pasta
  leftover vegetables, salads, casseroles
  whatever in the fridge needs to be eaten

- **Add seasonings**
  curry powder to chicken soup
  cloves to tomato soup
  wine, sherry, vermouth to mushroom soup

- **Add toppings**
  Parmesan cheese
  grated low-fat cheeses
  cottage cheese
  sesame seeds
  croutons

Pasta and Marathoners

Every marathoner regardless of language understands the word pasta. Pasta parties are universally enjoyed around the world. Pasta is popular not only pre-marathon, but also as a standard part of the training diet. Even marathoners who claim they can't cook manage to boil pasta in one shape or another. Some choose to eat pasta at least five nights of the week thinking it is a kind of superfood. Wrong.

Granted, pasta is carbohydrate-rich, quick and easy to cook, heart-healthy, economical, fun to eat, and enjoyed by just about every member of the family. But in terms of vitamins, minerals, and protein, plain pasta is a lackluster food. Here's some information to help you to place pasta in perspective.

Nutritional Value: Pasta is an excellent source of carbohydrates for muscle fuel and is the equivalent of "gas" for your engine. But plain pasta is a marginal source of vitamins and minerals, the "spark plugs" you need for top performance. Pasta is simply made from refined white flour—the same stuff you get in "wonder breads"—with a few vitamins added to replace those lost during processing. Even whole-wheat pastas offer little nutritional superiority, because wheat (and other grains in general) are better respected for their carbohydrate-value than their vitamins and minerals. Spinach and tomato pastas also are overrated since they contain relatively little spinach or tomato in comparison to having a serving of that vegetable along with the meal.

Pasta's nutritional value comes from the sauces:
- tomato sauce rich in vitamins A and C and potassium
- pesto-type sauces rich in vitamins A and C and potassium
- clam sauce rich in protein, zinc, and iron.

Be cautious with pasta smothered with butter, cream, or greasy meat sauces. Creamy, cheesy pastas can be artery-clogging nutritional nightmares.

Pasta and Protein: Pasta is popular not only for carbohydrates but also for being a vegetarian alternative to meat-based meals. However, many marathoners live on too much pasta and neglect their protein needs. For example, Joe,

Sharing enjoyable meals with your training partners is one of the pleasures of marathoning. Plan ahead!

an aspiring Olympian, thought his high-carbohydrate, low-fat diet of pasta and tomato sauce seven nights per week was top notch. He came to me wondering why he felt chronically tired and was not improving despite hard training.

The answer was simple. His limited diet was deficient in not only protein but also iron and zinc. Once he started to supplement the pasta with a variety of proteins, he started to feel better, run better, and recover better. He added to his tomato sauce a variety of protein-rich choices:

- 2–3 ounces of extra-lean ground beef or turkey:
- 1/4 cup of grated low-fat mozzarella cheese
- 1/2 cake tofu
- 1/2 cup canned, drained kidney beans
- 3 ounces tuna (one-half of a 6-ounce can)
- 1/2 cup of clams
- 1 cup of low-fat cottage cheese

Or, instead of adding protein to the sauce, he drank two glasses of low-fat milk with the meal.

Summary

If you are like many marathoners who struggle with eating well on a daily basis, you need to remember the following keys to a successful sports diet:

1. Eat appropriately sized meals on a regular schedule so that you won't get too hungry. Notice how your lunches and dinner deteriorate when you eat too little breakfast.
2. Spend your calories on a variety of wholesome foods at each meal; target at least three kinds of food per meal.
3. Pay attention to how much better you feel, run, and feel about yourself when you eat a well-balanced sports diet.

It's my opinion that getting too hungry is the biggest problem with most marathoners' diets. Hearty carbohydrate-based meals set the stage for a top-notch sports diet.

Mexican Baked Chicken with Beans

A spicy favorite that offers three food groups in one easy meal! When cooking for one, simply wrap one piece of chicken with 1/2 can of beans and 1/4 cup salsa in a piece of foil and bake in the toaster oven—no dishes to wash!
You can enjoy this as is, or along with rice and a green vegetable.

2 16 oz (480 g) cans pinto beans
4 pieces (6 oz raw; 180 g) chicken, boneless, skinless
1 cup (240 ml) salsa

Drain the beans and put them in the bottom of a baking dish.
Put the chicken on top; cover with salsa
Cover and bake at 350°F for 25 to 30 minutes. If desired, bake uncovered the last 10 minutes to thicken the pan juices.

Total calories: 1,600
Yield: 4 servings

One small serving: 400 calories
Carbohydrates: 36 g
Protein: 50 g
Fat: 6 g

From: *Nancy Clark's Sports Nutrition Guidebook, Third Edition* (Human Kinetics, 2003)

Chapter 4

Vitamins and Supplements for

**Vitamin pills are great,
but there's no substitute
for the real thing.**

*Jonathan Dietrich,
Washington, DC*

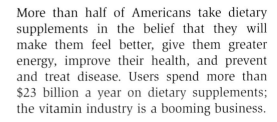

More than half of Americans take dietary supplements in the belief that they will make them feel better, give them greater energy, improve their health, and prevent and treat disease. Users spend more than $23 billion a year on dietary supplements; the vitamin industry is a booming business.

Vitamins are essential substances that your body can't make. They perform important jobs in your body, including helping to convert food into energy. (Vitamins do not provide energy, however; carbohydrates do.) Although a supplement is certainly a quick and easy safety net for hit-or-miss eating, I highly recommend that you first make the effort to "eat" your vitamins. As a hungry marathoner who requires more calories than the average person, you can easily consume large doses of vitamins in, let's say, a taller glass of orange juice or bigger pile of steamed broccoli. Chapter 1 has information about some of the best food sources of vitamins.

Because food consumption surveys suggest that many people fail to eat a well-balanced variety of wholesome foods, some runners and walkers may indeed suffer from marginal nutritional deficiencies, particularly those who:
- restrict calories
- eat a repetitive diet of rice cakes and apples
- skimp on fruits, vegetables, and dairy foods
- over-indulge in fats and sweets

Even marathoners who believe they eat well sometimes miss the mark. For example, one woman who took pride in her high-carbohydrate, low-fat diet (primarily bagels, bananas, pasta, and pretzels) ate too many carbohydrates at the exclusion of other foods (such as meats and dairy). She had a diet deficient in calcium, iron, zinc, and protein.

As a result of Americans' unbalanced food choices, should the general public be encouraged to take a supplement to compensate for poor eating habits? Not necessarily. Despite the rising popularity of supplements, many health organizations, including the American Heart Association and the National Institutes of Health, recommend food, not pills, for optimal nutrition. That's because food contains far more than just vitamins. It contains phytochemicals, fiber and other health-protective substances that are not in pills. Hence, the key to good health is to learn how to eat well despite a hectic lifestyle.

Let's take a look at some of what is and what is not known about nutritional supplements, and hopefully you'll see why spending more money on broccoli and orange juice rather than on pills and potions is the wiser bet. Whole foods offer protein, carbohydrates, fiber and phytochemicals—far more than just vitamins and minerals.

Vitamins were originally studied to determine the minimal amount of a nutrient required to prevent deficiency diseases, such as beriberi and scurvy. The recommended dietary allowances were developed to guide people towards an appropriate intake; they include a large safety margin. For example, in the United States, the Dietary Reference Intake (DRI) for vitamin C is 75 to 90 milligrams (women, men); this is four times the minimal amount needed to prevent the deficiency disease scurvy. The question remains unanswered: What is the optimal level of vitamins, not just to prevent *deficiency*, but to *enhance* health?

No amount of any supplement will compensate for a high-fat, hit-or-miss diet and stress-filled lifestyle. But supplements are indeed appropriate for certain populations, including:
- folic acid for pregnant women and women who *might* become pregnant (expectedly or unexpectedly) to prevent certain birth defects
- iron for vegetarians and women with heavy menstrual periods
- zinc and anti-oxidants for nonsmokers with macular degeneration (an eye disease)
- vitamin D and calcium for postmenopausal women for strong bones

To date, no studies have documented a physiological need for mega-doses of vitamins, even for marathoners or other athletes. Most athletes consume more than enough vitamins through their daily food intake.

Marathoners who eat vitamin-enriched energy bars and breakfast cereals, as well as other enriched grain foods, commonly consume far more vitamins than they realize. But take note: runners who eat primarily "all natural foods" from the health food stores miss out on the benefit of enriched foods. ("All natural foods" have no added vitamins or minerals, like iron.) That's one reason why the government acknowledges that some of our grains can appropriately come from enriched foods.

Food Offers More than Vitamins

Whole foods, such as fruits and vegetables, offer hundreds, perhaps thousands, of substances called *phytochemicals* that protect our health. These include:

- *protease inhibitors* in soybeans that may slow tumor growth
- *isoflavones* in dried beans that may reduce the risk of breast or ovarian cancer
- *isothiocyanates* in broccoli that may help block carcinogens from damaging a cell's DNA

These phytochemicals may explain why the cruciferous vegetables, such as broccoli, cabbage, and cauliflower, are thought to be protective against cancer, and onions and garlic are thought to be protective against heart disease.

While not a vitamin, omega-3 fish oil is another nutrient found in food that is powerfully health protective. The American Heart Association recommends that healthy people eat 12 ounces (two to three servings) of preferably oily fish, such as salmon and tuna, each week to provide the omega-3 fats that protect against heart disease. For non-fish eaters, flaxseed, walnuts and canola oil can be plant-based alternatives. Take heed: even fit marathoners are not immune from heart disease!

As you decide your nutritional fate, know that a diet based on a variety of wholesome foods is your best source of good nutrition. If you choose to take a supplement for its potential health-protective effects, be sure to do so in *addition to eating well*. Because researchers have yet to unravel the whole vitamin/health mystery, stay tuned and be sure to take care of your whole health. The phytochemicals, omega-3 fats and other unknown substances found in whole foods, but not in pills, may emerge as the winner.

Am I Sick? Am I Tired? Do I Need Vitamins?

Exercise energizes many people, enhancing their productivity, as well as relieving their stress. But some marathoners complain of chronic fatigue. They feel run down, dragged out, and overwhelmingly exhausted. If this sounds familiar, you may wonder if you are sick, overtired, or if something is wrong with your diet. You may wonder if taking vitamins would solve the problem.

Perhaps you can relate to Peter, a 39-year-old marathon runner, lawyer, and solo-chef who bemoaned, "I just don't take the time to eat right. My diet is awful. I rarely eat fruits or vegetables, to say nothing of a real meal. I think that poor nutrition is catching up with me. What vitamins should I take?"

Peter lived alone, hated to cook for just himself, and tended to survive on fast (and fatty) foods. He rarely ate breakfast, barely ate lunch, and always collapsed after a long day with a generous feast of a large deli sandwich, Chinese take-out, or pizza. He struggled to wake up in the morning, to stay awake during afternoon meetings, and to grind through his daily ten-mile run.

I evaluated Peter's diet, calculated that he required about 3,000 calories per day (700 to 800 calories per meal—breakfast, lunch #1, lunch #2, dinner), and suggested a few simple food changes that could result in higher energy, greater stamina, and better running. Trying to find some solutions to Peter's fatigue, I explored the following questions. Perhaps the answers will offer solutions for your energy problems.

- *Are you tired due to low blood sugar?* Peter skipped not only breakfast but also often missed lunch because he "didn't have time." He would doze off in the afternoon because he had low blood sugar. With zero calories to feed his brain, he ended up feeling sleepy.
  The solution was to choose to make time to eat. Just as he chose to sleep later in the morning, he could choose to stock trail mix (granola, nuts and raisins) at the office, so he could munch on that for his morning fuel. He could also choose to stop working for five or ten minutes to eat lunch.

- *Is your diet too low in carbohydrates?* Peter's fast-but-fatty food choices filled his stomach but left his muscles poorly fueled with inadequate glycogen to

- *Are you tired due to low blood sugar?* Peter skipped not only breakfast but also often missed lunch because he "didn't have time." He would doze off in the afternoon because he had low blood sugar. With zero calories to feed his brain, he ended up feeling sleepy.

  The solution was to choose to make time to eat. Just as he chose to sleep later in the morning, he could choose to stock trail mix (granola, nuts and raisins) at the office, so he could munch on that for his morning fuel. He could also choose to stop working for five or ten minutes to eat lunch.

- *Is your diet too low in carbohydrates?* Peter's fast-but-fatty food choices filled his stomach but left his muscles poorly fueled with inadequate glycogen to support his training program. Higher carbohydrate snacks and meals would not only would fuel his muscles but also help maintain a higher blood sugar level thereby providing energy for mental work, as well as physical exercise.

- *Are you iron-deficient and anemic?* Peter ate little red meat and consequently little iron, an important mineral in red blood cells that helps carry oxygen to exercising muscles. Iron-deficiency anemia can result in needless fatigue during exercise. I taught Peter how to boost his dietary iron intake, with or without meat. (See Chapter 6.) I also recommended he talk to his doctor about getting his blood tested (hemoglobin, hematocrit, ferritin, serum iron, and total iron-binding capacity) to rule out the question of anemia.

- *Are you getting enough sleep?* Peter's complaint about being chronically tired was justified because he was tired both mentally (from his intense job) and physically (from his strenuous training). He worked from 8 a.m. to 8 p.m. By the time he got home, ran, ate dinner, and "unwound," midnight had rolled around. The wake-up bell at 6:30 a.m. came all too soon—especially since Peter often had trouble falling asleep due to having eaten such a large dinner.

  To stay strong to the finish, be sure to eat your spinach. No vitamin pill can compensate for poor eating.

  I recommended that Peter try to get more sleep by eating lighter dinners (soup and sandwich, or even cereal), having bigger breakfasts, and scheduling his main meal at noon (low-fat

with family problems, to say nothing of the challenges of training for a marathon. Since he was feeling a bit helpless with this situation, I encouraged him to successfully control at least one aspect of his life—his diet. Simple dietary improvements could not only help him feel physically better but also mentally better about himself. This would be very energizing in itself.

If you answered "yes" to many of the questions I asked Peter, you may be able to resolve your fatigue with better eating, sleeping, and training habits—not with vitamin pills. Experiment with the simple food suggestions in this book. Before long, you may transform your current low-energy patterns into a food plan for success! Eating well is not as hard as you may think.

Summary

Your best bet for fighting fatigue is to be responsible with your food choices and nourish your body with the right balance of wholesome foods. Make the effort to eat a variety of foods and fluids from the different food groups every day. Eating marathoner's portions, you will consume not only the amounts of the vitamins and minerals you need, you will also be giving your body the *calories* it needs to prevent fatigue.

If you are tempted to take supplements for health insurance, do so only if you simultaneously choose to eat a healthful diet. Remember, no amount of supplements will compensate for an inadequate diet—but you will *always* win with good nutrition. Eat wisely, eat well!

For more information

Confusion abounds regarding dietary supplements, their safety, and their potential health benefits. Here are some websites that offer abundant information about vitamins and health. (You might need to do a search on "vitamins" or "fish oil" to find your topic of interest):
The American Heart Association:
www.americanheart.org
FDA's Center for Food Safety and Applied Nutrition
www.cfsan.fda.gov
National Library of Medicine:
www.nlm.nih.gov/medlineplus
The World's Healthiest Foods:
www.whfoods.org

A Super Salad

A colorful salad is a super way to boost your nutrient intake! Here's a suggestion for a super salad that is rich in not only vitamins, but also protein (to build muscles), carbs (to fuel muscles), fiber (to move food through your system) and healthful fats to help fight inflammation.
By eating a mix of nutrient-dense foods at most meals, you need not rely on vitamin pills to compensate for lousy eating.

In a large bowl, combine your choice of colorful salad vegetables, such as:

Spinach
Tomato
Red pepper
Yellow pepper
Carrot

Add protein and healthful fat:

Flaked tuna
Chopped walnuts
Olive oil-based salad dressing

Accompany with your choice of wholesome carbs:

Whole wheat English muffin
Toasted whole grain bread
Fresh rolls
Whole grain crackers

Chapter

Carbohydrate Confusion

Carbohydrates are how plants store energy. Hence, all plant foods—fruits, vegetables and grains—are carbohydrate-rich. As a marathoner, you need carbohydrates to fuel your muscles and feed your brain. You can consume carbs by eating bananas, (brown) rice, pasta, potatoes, honey, sports drinks, gum drops, even marshmallows. Obviously, you'll enhance your health if you choose carbs primarily from fruits, vegetables, and whole grains. But the sugary foods also offer the "gas" that fuels your muscles. The sugars just fail to offer any health protective vitamins or minerals.

While carb-bashers have long-established sugar as a dietary demon, starches have also gotten a bad rap thanks to Dr. Atkins and his high protein diet. Some marathoners, who had been happily enjoying bagels, pasta and pretzels as the foundation of their sports diet are shunning these excellent sources of muscle fuel. Instead, they choose egg whites, cottage cheese, soy shakes and protein-based foods. They also experience needless fatigue due to poorly fueled muscles.

Today, questions abound about the role of carbohydrates in the sports diet, as well as concerns about insulin (the hormone that helps carbs get stored in the muscles) and the glycemic effect of foods (that is, the rate at which a carbohdyrate enters the blood stream). The purpose of this chapter is to address carbohydrate confusion and provide some clarity for marthoners who want to eat wisely for good health, high energy, weight control and top performance.

Q: Are carbs fattening? Should I eat less of them?

A. *Carbohydrates are not inherently fattening. Excess calories are fattening.* Excess calories from carbohydrates (bread, bagels, pasta) are actually less fattening than are excess calories from fat (butter, mayonnaise, frying oils) because the body has to spend calories to convert excess carbohydrates into body fat. In comparison, the body easily converts excess calories of dietary fat into body fat. This means, if you are destined to be gluttonous but want to suffer the least weight gain, you might want to indulge in (high carb) frozen yogurt instead of (high fat) gourmet ice cream. See Chapter 15 for more information about how to lose weight and have energy to exercise.

Q. If carbs aren't fattening, why do high protein diets "work"?

A. *High protein diets seemingly "work" because:*

1. The dieter loses water weight. Carbs hold water in the muscles. For each ounce of carbohydrates you stored as glycogen, your body simultaneously stores about three ounces of water. When you deplete carbs during exercise, your body releases the water, and you experience a significant loss of weight that's mostly water, not fat.

2. People eliminate calories when they eliminate carbohydrates. For example, you might eliminate not only the baked potato (200 calories) but also two pats of butter (100 calories) on top of the potato—and this creates a calorie deficit.

3. Protein tends to be more satiating than carbohydrates. That is, protein (and fat) lingers longer in the stomach than do carbohydrates. Hence, having 200 calories of high-protein eggs for breakfast will satiate you longer than 200 calories in a high-carb bagel with jam. By curbing hunger, you have fewer urges to eat and can more easily restrict calories—that is, until you start to

crave carbs and over-eat them. (You know the scene: "Last chance to eat bagels before I go back on my diet, so I'd better eat them all now...")

The overwhelming reason high protein diets do NOT work is people fail to stay on them forever. Remember: You should never start a food program you do not want to maintain for the rest of your life. Do you really want to never eat breads, potato or crackers ever again? Your better option is to learn how to manage carbs, not avoid them.

Q. Is there a difference between the carbs in starchy foods (like breads) and the carbs in fruits, vegetables or candy?

A. *As far as your muscles are concerned, there is no difference. You can carbo-load on jelly beans, bananas or brown rice; they are biochemically similar.* Sugars and starches both offer the same amount of energy (4 calories per gram, or 16 calories per teaspoon) and both can be stored as glycogen in muscles or used for fuel by the brain (via the blood sugar).

The sugar in jelly beans is a simple compound, one or two molecules linked together. The starch in (brown) rice is a complex compound with hundreds to thousands of sugar molecules linked together. Sugars can convert into starches and starches can convert into sugars. For example:

*   When a banana is green (not ripe), it is starchy. As it gets older, it becomes sweeter. In fruits, the starch converts into sugar.
*   When peas are young, they are sweet. As they get older, they get starchier; in vegetables, the sugar converts into starch.

Grain foods (wheat, rice, corn, oats) also store their energy as complex strands of sugar molecules, a starch. The starch breaks down into individual sugar molecules (glucose) during digestion. Hence, your muscles don't care if you eat sugars or starches for fuel because they both digest into the same simple sugar: glucose.

The difference between sugars and starches comes in their nutritional value and impact on your health. Some sugars and starches are healthier than others. For example, the sugar in orange juice is accompanied by vitamin C, folate and potassium. The sugar in orange soda pop is devoid of vitamins and minerals; that's why it's described as "empty calories." The starch in whole wheat bread is accompanied by fiber and phytochemicals. The starch in white breads loses many health protective nutrients during the refining process.

Q. I've heard white bread is "poison." Do you agree?

A. *White bread offers lackluster nutrition, but it is not "poison" nor a "bad" food.* White bread can be balanced into an overall wholesome diet (as can pasta and other foods made from refined white flour). That is, if you have whole grain Wheaties for breakfast and brown rice for dinner, your diet can healthfully accommodate a sandwich made on white bread for lunch. White breads and food made from refined flour tend to be enriched with B-vitamins, iron and folate—all important nutrients for marathoners. According to the U.S. Dietary Guidelines, about half your grains can appropriately come from whole grains.

Q. Is sugar "evil?"

A. *Sugar is fuel, not evil.* While the sugar in oranges and other fruits is accompanied by important vitamins and minerals, the sugar, let's say, jelly beans, is devoid of nutritional value. In general, I suggest marathoners limit their refined sugar intake to about 10% of total calories. That's about 200 to 300 calories of sugar per day; 200 calories equates to a quart of Gatorade, two gels, 16 ounces of soda pop, or 10 jelly beans.

Most marathoners can handle sugar just fine. But for a few marathoners, sugar seems "evil" because it contributes to swings in blood sugar levels that can result in feeling lightheaded and shaky. If you are "sugar sensitive" and notice that sugar makes you feel poorly, choose sugar along with protein, such as jelly with peanut butter, apple with low-fat cheese, or fruit yogurt wth almonds.

Q. Should I avoid sugar pre-exercise?

A. *The best advice regarding pre-exercise sugar is for you to avoid the desire for sugar by having eaten appropriately prior to exercise.* For example, if you crave sugar before an afternoon training run, you could have prevented the desire for sugary, quick-energy foods by having eaten a bigger breakfast and lunch. Sugar cravings can be a sign you have gotten too hungry.

Note that sugar consumed during exercise is unlikely to contribute to a hypoglycemic reaction because muscles quickly use the sugar without the need for extra insulin. This includes sports drinks, gels, sports beans, gummy candies and other popular sugary choices. See Chapter 9 for more pre-exercise fueling tips.

Q. Should I choose foods based on their glycemic effect (that is, the rate at which they cause blood sugar to increase)?

A. *No; the glycemic response to a food varies from person to person, as well as from meal to meal (depending on the combinations of foods you eat).* You'll be better off experimenting with a variety of grains, fruits and vegetables to learn what food combinations settle well, satisfy your appetite and offer lasting energy. Wholesome, fiber-rich fruits, vegetables, beans and whole grains are wise food choices not because they tend to have a low gycemic effect (that is, cause a slow rise in blood sugar) but because they are nutrient-dense, can curb your appetite and may even help with weight management.

Building Carb-based Meals

As a marathoner, you should eat carbohydrates as the foundation of each meal. This can mean cereal for breakfast, sandwiches made on hearty bread for lunch, and for a dinner, a meal that includes a starch, such as pasta, potato, or rice. While you can get some carbs from fruits and veggies, most marathoners do not get enough carbs from these foods alone. Hence, they need the carb-boost from dinner starches. Here's some information to help you optimize your intake of these super-fuels.

Pasta for Carbohydrates

You don't have to be Italian to enjoy pasta! Marathoners around the globe enjoy fueling their muscles with a variety of pasta meals. You can choose from at least 26 shapes of pasta, ranging from angel hair to ziti. All the shapes are made from the same dough; some are tinted with vegetable juice (e.g., spinach, tomato). And all are easy to cook.

Tips for Cooking Pasta

- When trying to decide which shape of pasta to use for a meal, the rule of thumb is to use twisted and curved shapes (such as spirals and shells) with meaty, beany, and chunky sauces. The shape will trap more sauce than would the straight strands of spaghetti or linguini.
- If you want a quick-cooking pasta, choose angel hair, alphabets, and the little stars (stelline).
- To reduce cooking time, you can cook the pasta in half the amount of water (takes half as long to bring to a boil).
- Pasta is done when it starts to look opaque and is tender, yet firm to the teeth, or "al dente" as the Italians say.
- When done, drain the pasta into a colander set in the sink. Shake briefly to remove excess water, then return it to the cooking pot or to a warmed serving bowl. To prevent the pasta from sticking together as it cools, toss the pasta with a little olive or canola oil or tomato sauce.

Quick and Easy Ideas for Pasta Toppings

Tired of the same ol' spaghetti sauce, straight from the jar? Here are some quick and easy ideas for a change of pasta toppings:
- Salsa
- Salsa heated in the microwave, then mixed with cottage cheese
- Olive oil with red pepper flakes
- (Low-fat) Italian salad dressing mixed with a little Dijon mustard
- (Low-fat) salad dressings of your choice with steamed vegetables
- (Low-fat) sour cream and Italian seasonings
- Steamed, chopped broccoli (with Parmesan cheese)
- Parmesan cheese and a sprinkling of herbs (basil, oregano, Italian seasonings)
- Chicken breast sautéed with oil, garlic, onion, and basil
- Chili with kidney beans (and cheese)
- Lentil soup (thick)
- Spaghetti sauce with a spoonful of grape jelly (adds a "sweet 'n sour" taste)
- Spaghetti sauce with canned chicken or tuna, tofu cubes, canned beans, cottage cheese, ground beef or turkey (for protein)

Rice for Carbohydrates

Not all runners carbo-load on pasta. Rice is a fine alternative, preferably brown rice which retains the fiber-rich bran. Some marathoners enjoy rice for breakfast as an alternative to oatmeal.

Tips for Cooking Rice

- Because of its tough bran coat and germ, brown rice needs about 45 to 50 minutes to cook; white rice only takes about 20 to 30 minutes.
- Consider cooking rice in the morning while you are getting ready for work so that it will be waiting to be simply reheated when you get home.

- One-half cup of uncooked white or brown rice expands into about 1.5 cups of cooked rice. This is a reasonable portion (350 calories) for the average marathoner.
- When cooking rice, cook double amounts for leftovers that you can either freeze or refrigerate.

Quick and Easy Ideas for Meals with Rice

Cook rice in:
- Chicken or beef broth
- Mixture of orange or apple juice and water
- Water with seasonings: cinnamon, soy sauce, oregano, curry, chili powder, or whatever might nicely blend with the menu.

Top rice with:
- Leftover chili
- Low-fat or fat-free Italian dressing and mustard
- Toasted sesame seeds
- Steamed vegetables
- Chopped mushrooms and green peppers, either raw or sautéed
- Low-fat or fat-free sour cream, raisins, tuna, and curry powder
- Raisins, cinnamon, and applesauce

You can cook rice in a variety of ways. Here are two popular methods:

Boiled rice #1
- Bring a saucepan of water to a full boil.
- Stir in 1/3 to 1/2 cup of rice per person plus 1 to 2 teaspoons salt, as desired.
- Simmer about 20 minutes, or until a grain of rice is tender when you bite into it.
- Drain into a colander, rinse it under hot tap water to remove the sticky starch, and put it back into the saucepan.
- Keep the rice warm over low heat, fluffing it with a fork.

Boiled rice #2

This method retains more of the vitamins that otherwise get lost into the cooking water.

- For each one cup of rice, put two cups of water into a saucepan, and a teaspoon salt, as desired.
- Bring to a boil, then cover and turn the heat down low.
- Let the rice cook undisturbed until it is tender and all the water has been absorbed.
- Stir gently with a fork. Do not over-stir, which may result in a gluey mess.

Potatoes for Carbohydrates

Potatoes are a nutritious source of carbohydrates, more so than plain pasta or rice. A large baking potato offers more than half the vitamin C you need for the day, plus all the potassium you'd lose in three hours of sweaty exercise. A sweet potato offers even more health benefits.

Some marathoners enjoy baked potatoes for not only meals but also snacks. Pre-baked, you can eat them as you might eat a piece of fruit before or after workouts. The standard "restaurant size" potato generally has about 200 calories, similar to an energy bar.

Here are some tips for enjoying potatoes in your sports diet:

- Potatoes come in different varieties, with some varieties best suited for baking (russets), others for boiling (red or white rounds). Ask the produce manager at your grocery store for guidance.
- Potatoes are best stored in a cool place that is well ventilated, such as your cellar. Do not refrigerate potatoes because they will become sweet and off-colored.
- Rather than peel the skin (a good source of fiber), scrub the skin well, cook it, and eat it, skin and all. Even mashed potatoes can be made unpeeled!
- To bake a potato in the oven, allow about 40 minutes at 400°F for a medium potato, closer to an hour for a large potato. Because potatoes can be baked at any temperature, you can simply adjust the cooking time to whatever else is in the oven.
- The potato is baked enough when you can easily pierce it with a fork.
- To cook a potato in the microwave oven, prick the skin in several places with a fork, place it on some paper towels in the microwave, and zap it for about 4 minutes if it is medium-sized, 6 to 10 minutes if large. (Cooking time will vary according to the size of the potato, the power of your oven, and the number of potatoes being cooked.) Turn the potato over halfway through cooking. Remove the potato from the oven, wrap it in a towel and allow it to finish cooking for about 3 to 5 minutes.

Quick and Easy Ideas for Potato Toppings

To spice up your potato, try the following toppings:
- (Low-fat) salad dressing
- (Low-fat) sour cream, chopped onion, and grated low-fat cheddar cheese
- Cottage cheese and garlic powder
- Cottage cheese and salsa
- Milk mashed into the potato
- Plain yogurt
- Mustard or ketchup
- Mustard and Worcestershire sauce
- Vinegar and flavored vinegars
- Soy sauce
- Pesto
- Chopped chives and green onion
- Herbs, such as dill, parsley, chopped chives
- Steamed broccoli or other cooked vegetables
- Chopped jalapeno peppers
- Lentils or lentil soup
- Soup broth
- Applesauce

Summary

Carbohydrates should not be a source of confusion. To the contrary: wholesome carbs—fruits, vegetables, grains—clearly should be the foundation of your sports diet. And, if desired, refined carbs—soda pop, sugar, sports drinks—can be consumed in moderation. As a marathoner, you may be unable to get adequate carbs from fruits and veggies to fuel your muscles, so be sure to include some pasta, potatoes, rice or other starches in your dinner menu. By "carbo-loading" every day, your muscles will have the fuel they need to train at their best, and this will help you compete at your best.

Hummus

Hummus is made with chick peas (garbanzo beans)—an excellent source of not only carbs but also a good source of protein. Enjoy hummus as:
- a dip with pita bread or baby carrots
- a sandwich spread along with turkey
- a roll-up with shredded veggies

The secret ingredient in hummus is tahini—sesame paste. You can buy tahini in the ethnic food section of supermarkets or whole food stores. (Hint: Enjoy the leftover tahini on pasta!)

- 1 16 oz (480 g) can chick peas
- 1 tablespoon (15 ml) lemon juice
- 1 clove garlic (or 1/4 tsp/1 g garlic powder) to taste
- 2 tablespoons (30 g) tahini (or peanut butter can be substituted)
- salt and pepper, as desired

Optional: dash of cayenne; 1 tablespoon parsley; 1/2 teaspoon cumin

- Drain the chick peas, saving 1/4 cup (60 ml) of the liquid.
- In a blender or food processor, mix the chick-peas, 1/4 cup (60 ml) liquid, lemon juice, garlic, tahini, and seasonings.
- Blend until smooth. If you don't have a blender, mash the chick peas with the back of a fork.
- Serve with pita bread or as a dip for raw vegetables.

Total calories: 625	Carbohydrate	11 g
8 servings	Protein	3 g
One serving: 80 calories	Fat	3 g

Chapter 6

Protein for Marathoners

Due to the influence of protein supplement advertisements, as well as the Atkins Diet (that wrongly deems carbohydrates as fattening and protein as slimming), many marathoners have made protein the foundation of their sports diets. They believe a strong protein intake will boost their power and strength; they eat protein bars or shakes before their long training runs. Too bad! There's little doubt that carbs are the preferred source of fuel for muscles.

Marathoners should eat adequate, but not excess, lean sources of protein as an accompaniment to a carbohydrate-based sports diet. Your body needs protein to:
- build and repair muscles
- make red blood cells
- make enzymes and hormones
- grow hair and fingernails

About 10 to 15 percent of your calories should come from protein; that translates into a little bit of protein at each meal. Some marathoners eat more than that; other eat less. Here are some tips to consuming the right amount of protein to optimize performance and recovery.

How Much Protein Is Enough?

The current recommended daily allowance (RDA) for protein is 0.4 grams of protein per pound of body weight (0.8 gm/kg). This RDA was based on *sedentary* college students. Because marathoners have a slightly higher protein need, an adequate and safe protein intake is about 0.5 to 0.8 grams of protein per pound of body weight (1.0 to 1.6 gm/kg). Growing teenagers, athletes building new muscles, marathoners doing lots of long runs, or dieters who restrict calories (which results in protein being used for fueling rather than maintaining muscles), should target the higher end of the protein range.

> **Be sure to include enough protein in your training diet! I used to eat too many carbs and too little protein, and my performance suffered. Now I make sure to include some chicken or fish with my salads for dinner, and dairy with my breakfast each day. Once I started to pay attention to my protein intake, my recovery after long runs improved dramatically.**
>
> *Kip Parker, Atlanta, GA*

How Much Protein Is Too Little?

Some marathoners, being health conscious, have reduced their meat (and saturated fat) intake, with hopes of reducing their risk of heart disease. While reducing fatty meat intake is a good idea, some of these non-meat eaters have totally cut out animal proteins; they call themselves "vegetarians" when they are really just "non-meat eaters" because they have failed to add any plant proteins to their daily meals. They live on fruit, vegetables, and pasta. The result is a protein-deficient diet.

If you aspire to a vegetarian diet and have stopped eating meats, make sure you are addressing your overall protein needs. You should consume a small amount

How to Balance Your Protein Intake

If you wonder if you are eating too little (or too much) protein, you can estimate your daily protein needs by multiplying your weight (or a good weight for your body) by 0.5 to 0.75 grams of protein per pound (1.0 to 1.5 g Pro/kg).

Weight	Protein
lbs (kg)	(grams/day)
100 (45)	50-80
120 (55)	60-90
150 (68)	75-100
170 (77)	85-115

Use food labels and the following chart to calculate your protein intake. Pay close attention to portion sizes!

Approximate Protein Content of Some Commonly Eaten Foods

Animal Proteins	Protein (grams)
Beef, 4 oz, (120g) cooked*	32
Chicken breast, small 4 oz cooked	32
Tuna, 1 can (6.5 ounces)	40
Meat, fish, poultry, 1 oz. (30 g) cooked	7-8
Egg, 1	7
Egg white, 1	3

*4 ounces cooked = size of deck of cards
4 ounces cooked = 5 to 6 ounces raw

Plant Proteins	
Lentils, beans, 1/2 cup (100 g)	7
Baked beans, 1/2 cup (130 g)	7
Peanut butter, 2 tablespoons (30 g)	8
Tofu, 1/4 cake firm (4 oz, 120 g)	8
Soy milk, 1 cup (240 ml)	7

Dairy Products	
Milk, yogurt, 1 cup (240 ml)	8
Cheese, 1 ounce (30 g)	8
Cheese, 1 slice American (2/3 oz; 20 g)	6
Cottage cheese, 1/3 cup (75 g)	8
Milk powder, 1/4 cup (30 g)	8

Breads, Cereals, Grains	
Bread, 1 slice (30 g)	2
Cold cereal, 1 ounce (30 g)	2
Oatmeal, 1/3 cup dry (30 g), or 1 cup cooked	5
Rice, 1/3 cup dry (55 g), or 1 cup cooked	4
Pasta, 2 ounces dry (60 g), or 1 cup cooked	7

Starchy Vegetables	
Peas, carrots, 1/2 cup (80 g) cooked	2
Corn, 1/2 cup cooked (80 g)	2
Beets, 1/2 cup cooked (80)	2
Winter squash, 1/2 cup (100 g)	2
Potato, 1 small (125 g)	2

Fruits, Watery Vegetables

Negligible amounts of protein. Most fruits and vegetables have only small amounts of protein. They may contribute a total of 5 to 10 grams protein per day, depending on how much you eat.

Quick and Easy Meatless Meals

Here a few ideas to help you with a meat-free diet that has adequate protein.

Breakfast:
- Cold cereal (preferably iron-enriched, as noted on the label): Top with (soy) milk or yogurt and sprinkled with a few nuts.
- Oatmeal, oat bran, and other hot cereals: Add peanut butter, almonds or other nuts, and/or powdered milk.
- Toast, bagels: Top with low-fat cheese, cottage cheese, or peanut butter.

Snacks:
- Assorted nuts
- Peanut butter on rice cakes or crackers
- Yogurt (Note: Frozen yogurt has only 4 grams of protein per cup, as compared to 8 grams of protein in regular yogurt.)

Lunch and Dinner:
- Salads: Add tofu, chick peas, three-bean salad, marinated kidney beans, cottage cheese, sunflower seeds, chopped nuts.
- Protein-rich salad dressing: Add salad seasonings to plain yogurt, or blenderized tofu or cottage cheese (diluted with milk or yogurt).
- Spaghetti sauce: Add diced tofu and/or canned, drained kidney beans.
- Pasta: Choose protein-enriched pastas that offer 13 grams of protein per cup (140 g), as compared to 8 grams in regular pasta. Top with grated part-skim mozzarella cheese.
- Potato: Bake or microwave, then top with canned beans, baked beans, or low-fat cottage cheese.
- Hearty soups: Choose lentil, split pea, bean, and minestrone.
- Hummus: Try with pita or tortillas.
- Cheese pizza: A protein-rich fast food, half of a 12-inch pizza has about 40 grams of protein.

of protein-containing food (milk, peanut butter, hummus, etc.) at each meal. Otherwise, you'll feel the results of a protein imbalance: chronic fatigue, anemia, lack of improvement, muscle wasting, and an overall run-down feeling.

Marathoners with big appetites can more easily consume adequate protein than can calorie-conscious dieters. That is, if you eat only a smidgen of peanut butter on a lunchtime sandwich and a sprinkling of garbanzo beans on a dinner salad, you likely fall short of meeting the approximate 50–70 grams of protein needed by active women and 70–90 grams of protein needed by men. See the worksheet "How to balance your protein intake" (page 59) to help you calculate your protein needs.

Note that a protein-deficient diet can also lack iron (prevents anemia) and zinc (helps with healing). I will discuss these minerals later.

The key to eating a high quality vegetarian diet is to eat a variety of foods that contain a variety of the eight essential amino acids needed for building protein. You can do that by simply eating a variety of grains, beans, legumes, nuts, seeds, soy and dairy products during meals and snacks over the course of the day.

Beans

For vegetarian marathoners, beans are not only a good source of protein, but also of carbohydrates, B-vitamins (such as folic acid), and fiber. When added to an overall low-fat diet, they may help lower elevated blood cholesterol levels. The problem with beans is flatulence; some runners become gas propelled! If beans cause you intestinal problems, eat small amounts. If you cook your own beans, be sure to soak them long enough before cooking. You can also try Beano, a product that when added to beans helps reduce gas formation.

If you want to learn how to include more beans in your sports diet, here are a few suggestions:

- Sauté garlic and onions in a little oil; add canned, drained beans (whole or mashed); and heat together.
- Add beans to salads, spaghetti sauce, soups, and stews for a protein booster.
- In a blender, mix black beans, salsa and cheese. Heat in the microwave and use as a dip or on top of tortillas or potatoes.

Red Meat: Eat or Avoid?

Red meats, such as beef and lamb, are indisputably excellent sources of high-quality protein. They are also rich in iron and zinc, two minerals important for optimal health and athletic performance. Yet, some meat-eating marathoners are a bit unsure if eating red meat is a positive addition to their sports diet. If you wonder whether or not you should eat or avoid red meat, know that the answer is not a simple yes or no but rather a weighing of nutrition facts, ethical concerns, personal values, and dedication to making appropriate food choices. Yes, you can get the nutrients needed to support your sports program from non-red-meat sources, but you have to make the effort to do so. The following facts can help you decide if tucking two to four small (3-4 ounce) portions of red meat per week into your meals might enhance the quality of your diet.

It is easy to get enough carbs, but getting enough protein makes a big difference in my day-to-day performance.

Jonathan Dietrich, Washington, DC

Meat and cholesterol: Meat, like chicken, fish, and other animal products, contains cholesterol because cholesterol is a part of animal cells; plant cells contain no cholesterol. Most animal proteins have similar cholesterol values: 70–80 milligrams of cholesterol per four-ounce serving of red meat, poultry, and fish.

Given that the American Heart Association recommends that healthy people with normal blood cholesterol levels eat less than 300 milligrams of cholesterol per day, small portions of red meat can certainly fit those requirements. Marathoners who know their blood cholesterol number can best make personalized dietary decisions about how much cholesterol is appropriate for their bodies.

Note that the cholesterol content of meat is of less concern than the fat content. Fatty meats, such as greasy hamburgers, pepperoni, juicy steaks, and sausage, are the real dietary no-nos. Lean meats—London broil, extra-lean hamburger, top round roast beef—can fit into a heart-healthy sports diet in appropriate amounts.

Chicken Again?

Chicken has less saturated fat than many cuts of red meat, hence it can be a good alternative for dinner. But if you are tired of eating yet another boring chicken breast, here are some simple ideas to spice it up:

- Spread with mustard and sprinkle with Parmesan cheese
- Spread with honey and sprinkle with curry powder
- Marinate for an hour or overnight in Italian dressing
- Spread with honey mustard

Place in baking pan (lined with foil for easy clean up) and bake uncovered at 350°F (175°C) for 20 to 30 minutes.

Meat and iron: Adequate iron in your sports diet is important to prevent anemia. Without question, the iron in red meat is more easily absorbed than that in popular vegetarian sources of iron (e.g., beans, raisins, spinach). In a study of eighteen women runners who consumed the recommended daily allowance for iron, eight of the nine women who ate no red meat (but did eat chicken and fish) had depleted iron stores as compared to only two of the nine red-meat eaters.

If you eat an iron-poor diet and are tempted to simply take an iron supplement, note that animal iron is absorbed better the iron in a pill. But any iron is better than no iron.

Meat and zinc: Zinc is important for healing both the minor damage that occurs with daily training, as well as major injuries and ailments. It is best found in iron-rich foods (e.g., red meat). Diets deficient in iron may

---

How to Boost Your Iron Intake

- The recommended intake for iron is 8 milligrams for men and 18 milligrams for women per day. Women have higher iron needs to replace the iron lost from menstrual bleeding. Women who are post-menopausal require only 8 milligrams of iron per day.
- Iron from animal products is absorbed better than that from plant products.
- A source of vitamin C at each meal enhances iron absorption.

Animal Sources (best absorbed)	Iron (mg)
Beef, 4 oz (120 g) cooked	2
Pork, 4 oz (120 g)	1
Chicken breast, 4 oz (120 g)	1
Chicken leg, 4 oz (120 g)	1.5
Salmon, 4 oz (120 g)	1

Fruits

Prunes, 5	1
Raisins, 1/3 cup (45 g)	1

Vegetables

Spinach, 1/2 cup (100 g) cooked	3
Broccoli, 1 cup (180 g) cooked	1

Beans

Kidney, 1/2 cup (130 g)	2.5
Tofu, 1/2 cake (120 g)	2

Grains

Cereal, 100% iron fortified 1 oz (30 g)	18
Spaghetti, 1 cup cooked (140 g)	2
Bread, 1 oz (30 g) slice, enriched	1

Other

Molasses, blackstrap, 1 tablespoon (15 g)	3.5
Wheat germ, 1/4 cup (30 g)	2

then also be deficient in zinc. Like iron, the zinc in animal products is absorbed better than that in vegetable foods or supplements.

Meat and amenorrhea: Female runners who have amenorrhea and have stopped getting their menstrual period commonly eat no red meat. In one study, none of the amenorrheic runners ate red meat as compared to 44 percent of the runners with regular menses.

The question remains unanswered: Are these amenorrheic athletes simply protein deficient or is there a meat factor that affects the hormones involved with menstruation? Amenorrhea is a sign of poor health and loss of menses coincides with a higher rate of stress fractures. Hence, women who do not menstruate should carefully evaluate the adequacy of their diet. A sports dietitian can help them determine if their diet includes adequate protein, calories, and other nutritiens. Refer to Chapter 16 for more information.

How to Boost Your Zinc Intake

- The recommended intake for zinc is 8 milligrams for women and 11 milligrams for men per day.
- Animal foods, including seafood, are the best sources of zinc.

Animal Sources	Zinc (mg)
Beef, tenderloin, 4 ounces (120 g)	7
Chicken leg, 4 ounces (120 g)	3.5
Pork loin, 4 ounces (120 g)	3
Chicken breast, 4 ounces (120 g)	1
Cheese, 1 ounce (30 g)	1
Milk, 1 cup (240 ml)	1
Oysters, 6 medium (3 oz; 90 g)	75 (!)
Tuna, 1 can (6 oz; 170 g)	2
Clams, 9 small (3 oz; 90 g)	1

Plant Sources	
Wheat germ, 1/4 cup (30 g)	3.5
Lentils, 1 cup (200 g)	2.5
Almonds, 1 oz (30 g)	1
Garbanzo beans, 1/2 cup (100 g)	1
Spinach, 1 cup (200 g) cooked	0.7
Peanut butter, 1 tablespoon (15 g)	0.5
Bread, 1 slice (30 g), whole wheat	0.5

Hormones in meats: Fears abound regarding hormones given to cattle to enhance their growth. The U.S. Department of Agriculture claims the amount of hormones used is far less than one might get in a birth control pill, or even in a cup of coleslaw, for that matter. You can always buy "all-natural" meat to be on the safe side.

Fish: A Super-protein

The protein in fish is among the most healthful animal sources of protein. That's because fish is low in saturated fat, the kind of fat that is associated with heart disease. And, fish is rich in omega-3 fat, the good fat that makes human blood less likely to form clots that cause heart attacks and strokes. The American Heart Association (AHA) recommends eating two fish meals per week, particularly meals with oily fish, such as trout, wild or canned salmon, light tuna, sardines and herring.

Why Chicken Has Light and Dark Meat

The white and dark meat in chicken (and turkey) is a handy example of the two kinds of muscle fibers that help you exercise:
- Fast-twitch fibers (white breast meat) are used for quick bursts of energy
- Slow-twitch fibers (dark leg, thigh, and wing meat) function best for endurance exercise.

Elite marathon runners tend to have the right combination of both—a high proportion of slow-twitch fibers for the long run, but also enough fast-twitch fibers for the sprint to the finish.

Slow-twitch muscles, more so than fast-twitch, rely on fat for fuel. This is why dark meat contains more fat than white meat. On the plus side, dark meat also contains more nutrients—iron, zinc, and B-vitamins, many of the same nutrients found in red meats.

Chicken, without skin, 4 oz (120) cooked	Calories	Fat (g)	Iron (g)
Breast, white meat	180	4	1.2
Thigh, dark meat	235	12	1.5
Leg, dark meat	200	9	1.3

If you do not eat red meats, you might want to include more dark meat from chicken or turkey in your sports diet. For the small price of a few grams of fat, you'll get more nutritional value. If you want to cut back on fat, eliminate the skin—the fattiest part of poultry.

Eating fish comes with risks related to mercury and PCBs (polychlorinated biphenyls). The Food and Drug Administration (FDA) and the Environmental Protection Agency (EPA) advise women who may become pregnant or who currently are pregnant or breast feeding (as well as young children) to avoid the fish highest in mercury (shark, swordfish, king mackerel (ono), tilefish). Large amounts of methylmercury can harm an unborn or young child's developing nervous system, resulting in problems with IQ, attention, reading, and memory. But everyone—including pregnant women—can safely enjoy up to twelve ounces (two or three fish meals) per week of low-mercury fish and shellfish: shrimp, salmon, pollock, catfish, and canned light tuna.

The health benefits of eating fish generally far outweight the risks. But take note: if you are into sport-fishing, sushi-eating, having tuna for lunch every day, and enjoying high-mercury fish several times a week, the mercury can accumulate in your body and might create health problems. The trick to eating fish is to eat it in moderation and to consume a variety of different fish, with a focus on the smaller fish. Each week, enjoy a meal with oily fish (salmon, blue fish) and another with low-mercury fish (pollock, sole.) Be moderate, and you'll get hooked on good health.

Strong musles are important for marathon success. Be sure to get enough protein by eating protein-rich foods at two meals per day.

Protein Bars

When you are on the run and grabbing meals, a protein bar can be a convenient way to get hassle-free, low-fat protein. But because it is an manufactured food, it lacks the wholesome goodness and yet-unidentified compounds that nature puts in all natural sources of protein. Most protein bars include protein from whey or casein (milk is about 20% whey, 80% casein), soy and/or egg—all of which are excellent sources of amino acids. Some of the bars are handy snacks, others are hefty enough to be a meal replacement. They fall into the category of "convenient" but not "necessary."

Cooking Fish

Although cooking fish is simple, many marathoners eat fish only in restaurants because they don't know how to cook it. My advice: learn how to cook fish so you'll enjoy it more often as a great source of protein with a bonus of health-protective fish oils.

Here are some fish tips:
- Buy fresh fish that has no "fishy" odor. Ask to smell the fish before purchasing it. Fishy odor comes only with age and bacterial contamination.
- To rid your hands of any fishy smell, rub them with lemon juice or vinegar, then wash them.
- Seasonings that go well with fish include lemon, dill, basil, rosemary, and parsley (and paprika for color).
- When grilling, sauteing or broiling fish, allow 10 minutes cooking time per inch of thickness. Fold thin parts under to make the fish as even a thickness as possible. As fish cooks, the flesh turns from translucent to opaque white, similar to egg whites.
- To test for doneness, gently pull the fish apart with a fork. It should flake easily and no longer be translucent. Do not overcook fish. Perfectly cooked fish is moist and has a delicate flavor, unlike overcooked fish that is dry and tasteless.
- If possible, cook fish in its serving dish (or in foil); fish is fragile and more attractive the less it is handled.

Summary

Lean meat is a convenient, nutrient-dense sports food. The fat in greasy meats, not the red meat itself, is the primary health culprit. Chicken and fish are lower fat alternatives, with fish being the healthiest choice of all. If you prefer a vegetarian diet, just be sure to have a protein-rich food with each meal. "Vegetarians" who simply eliminate meat and make no effort to include alternate plant sources of protein, iron, and zinc can suffer from dietary deficiencies that hurt their sports performance. Protein bars can be a handy "emergency food" when you are eating on the run and your protein needs would otherwise be neglected.

Fish Florentine

Here's a simple fish recipe that's easy even for "non cooks." It goes nicely with rice or crusty whole grain rolls.

1 10-ounce bag (300 g) fresh spinach, washed or 1 10-ounce box frozen chopped spinach, thawed and drained
1/2 cup (2 ounces; 30 g) shredded mozzarella cheese
1 lb (16 ounces; 480 g) fish fillets
Salt, pepper and lemon juice, as desired

TO COOK IN THE OVEN
1. Preheat the ofen to 400°F (200°C).
2. Layer the spinach on the bottom of a deep baking dish.
3. Top with the fish and sprinkle with cheese. Season as desired.
4. Cover loosely and bake for 20 minutes or until the fish flakes easily.

MICROWAVE OPTION
1. Divide the spinach into two microwavable plates.
2. Top with the fish and sprinkle with cheese. Season as desired.
3. Cover loosely (using toothpicks to hold the covering away from the cheese, if necessary). Microwave on high for about 2 to 4 minutes (depending on the thickness of the fish) or until the fish flakes easily.

Total calories: 560 (made with white fish)
Calories per serving: 280

One serving:
Carbohydrates: 6 g
Protein: 50 g
Fat: 6 g

Chapter 7

Fats and Your Sports Diet

Eat fat, get fat. Eat fat, clog your arteries. Eat fat, have a heart attack. Eat fat, run slow. I'm sure you've heard this anti-fat chatter. While there is an element of truth in some of these statements, there is also room for more education. Let's look at the whole picture.

While dietary fat used to be considered bad, we now know that all fats are not created equal. The hard, saturated fat in beef, butter and cheese is the "bad" fat, as are the trans (partially hydrogenated) fats in commercially baked goods. The soft, liquid polyunsaturated and monounsaturated fats in fish, olives and nuts are the "good" fats, an essential nutrient needed for overall good health. Hence, there's no need to avoid all fat like the plague.

Olive oil, for example, is health-protective; it is the foundation of the acclaimed heart-healthy Mediterranean diet. For centuries, native Italians and Greeks have enjoyed good health and a 40-percent fat diet. In general, I recommend that healthy marathoners target a sports diet with about 25 percent of the calories from (primarily healthful) fat. This:
- is in keeping with the American Heart Association's recommendation for a diet with 25 to 35 percent of the calories from fat.
- allows for adequate calories from carbohydrates (55–65 percent of total calories) and proteins (10–15 percent of total calories).
- provides fat-soluble vitamins, such as vitamin E (an anti-oxidant thought to have a health-protective effect).
- allows for easier participation in life (i.e., eating at a party, enjoying a cookie guilt-free).

How does 25 percent fat translate into food? Let's say you have 1,800 calories a day in your calorie budget (this would be a reducing diet for most female marathoners):

25 x 1,800 total calories = 450 calories a day of fat.

Because there are 9 calories per gram of fat, divide 450 calories by 9:

450 calories / 9 calories per gram = 50 grams of fat in your daily fat budget.

A 25-percent-fat diet includes a reasonable amount of fat and lets you enjoy a little fat at each meal. Preferably, you'll choose fats that have positive health value such as olive oil, salmon and other oily fish, all-natural peanut butter, low-fat cheese, nuts, and tuna with light mayonnaise. But, if you do have the occasional hankering for a big burger with 25 grams of fat and 500 calories, simply fit it into your day's fat and calorie budget *and balance the rest of the day's meals.* (Refer to Chapter 14 to determine your calorie needs.)

Fat Guidelines

The following guidelines can help you appropriately budget fat into your food plan.

Calories per day	Fat grams per day (for 25-percent-fat diet)
1,600	45
1,800	50
2,000	55
2,200	60
2,400	65

Fat Content of Some Common Foods

Food	Serving size	Fat (grams)	Calories
Dairy products			
Milk, whole (3 1/2% fat)	1 cup (240 ml)	8	150
Reduced-fat (2 1/2 fat)	"	5	120
Low-fat (1 1/2, 1/2% fat)	"	2	100
Fat-free (0% fat)	"	–	80
Cheese			
Cheddar	1 oz (30 g)	9	110
Reduced-fat	"	5	90
Mozzarella, part-skim	"	5	80
Cottage cheese (4% fat)	1/2 cup (120 g)	5	120
Low-fat cottage cheese (2% fat)	"	2	90
Cream cheese	1 oz (2 tbsp; 30 g)	10	100
Light	"	5	60
Ice cream, gourmet	1/2 cup (100 g)	15	250
Standard	" (80 g)	8	150
Light	" (70 g)	3	110
Frozen yogurt, low-fat	" (70 g)	2	120
Fat-free	" (90 g)	–	100
Animal proteins			
Beef, regular hamburger	4 oz cooked (120 g)	24	330
Flank steak	"	12	235
Eye of round	"	6	200

Food	Amount	Fat (g)	Calories
Chicken, breast, no skin	4 oz cooked (120 g)	5	200
thigh, no skin	"	11	235
Fish, haddock	4 oz cooked (120 g)	1	125
Swordfish	"	6	175

Vegetable proteins

Food	Amount	Fat (g)	Calories
Beans, kidney	1/2 C cooked (100 g)	--	110
Lentils	"	--	110
Tofu	4 oz (120 g)	5	90
Peanut butter	1 tbsp (15 g)	8	95

Fats

Food	Amount	Fat (g)	Calories
Butter	1 tbsp (15 g)	12	108
Margarine	"	11	102
Oil, olive	"	13	120
Mayonnaise	"	11	100

Grains

Food	Amount	Fat (g)	Calories
Bread, whole wheat	1 large slice (30 g)	1	90
Crackers, Saltines	5	2	60
Ritz	4	4	70
Rice cakes	1		35
Cereal, shredded wheat	1 oz (2/3 cup; 30 g)	–	90
Granola	1 oz (1/4 cup; 30 g)	6	130
Oatmeal	1 oz (1/3 cup; 30 g) dry	2	100
Spaghetti, plain	2 oz. dry (1 cup cooked; 140 g)	1	210
Rice	2 oz dry (1 cup cooked; 160 g)	–	200

Fast foods

Food	Amount	Fat (g)	Calories
Big Mac	1	30	560
Egg McMuffin	1	12	300
French fries	small	13	250
KFC Fried chicken	breast	19	380
Pizza, cheese	1 slice, large	10 – 13	250

Snacks, Treats

Cookie, Chips Ahoy	1 (1/2 oz; 15)	2	50
Fig Newton	1 (1/2 oz; 15 g)	1	60
Brownie, from mix	1 small	5	140
Graham crackers	2 squares	1	60
Potato chips	1 oz (about 18 chips)	9	150
Pretzels	1 oz (30 g)	1	110
Milky Way	1.75 oz bar (50 g)	8	220
M&Ms w/ peanuts	1.75 oz (50 g) bag	13	250
Reese's Peanut Butter Cups	1.6 oz (2 cups; 45 g)	15	280

Fruits and Vegetables

Most varieties	negligible fat

Fear of Fat

Without question, fat imparts a tempting taste, texture, and aroma and helps make food taste great. That's why fatty foods can be hard to resist and are enjoyed to excess. Although excess fat calories can easily turn into body fat, note the "eat fat, get fat" theory is false. Many active people eat appropriate amounts of fat and stay thin. They simply don't *overeat* calories.

If you are weight-conscious and obsess about every gram of fat to the extent you have a fat phobia, your fear of fat may be exaggerated! A little fat can actually aid in weight reduction because it takes longer to empty from the stomach—and offers that nice feeling of being satisfied after a meal. For example, you may have less desire to keep munching on, let's say, yet another rice cake if you start by eating a rice cake with a little peanut butter.

Believe it or not, but many of my clients have lost body fat after they reintroduced an appropriate amount of dietary fat back into their fat-free regimen. Refer to the weight reduction information in Chapter 15 for additional help with resolving your "eat fat, get fat" fears.

As a marathoner, you want to include a little fat in each meal to not only help absorb certain vitamins but also to enhance performance. Runners who boosted their intake of healthful fat from 17% of calories to 30% of calories were not only able to run longer but also had less inflammation afterwards. Fat is certainly NOT a four letter word!

Summary

Marathoners who include some fat in their daily training diet perform better than those who try to exclude fat. Obviously, choosing more of the *healthful* fats—olive oil, canola oil, nuts, peanut butter, salmon—is preferable to loading up on the fat from buttery cookies, greasy burgers, and gourmet ice cream. But all fats eaten in moderation can be balanced into an overall healthful and carbohydrate-rich sports diet.

Oven French Fries

Fast foods, such as french fries, although tempting to some marathoners, are not the best choices for your weight gain diet. Here's a tasty alternative to commercial fries; these are made with either olive or canola oil that protects your health rather than clog your arteries.

Per serving:

1 large baking potato, cleaned, unpeeled
1 teaspoon oil, preferably canola or olive
Salt and pepper to taste

Optional:
Red pepper flakes
Dried basil
Oregano
Minced garlic
Parmesan cheese

1. Cut each potato lengthwise into 10 or 12 pieces. Place in a large bowl; cover with cold water and let stand for 15 to 20 minutes. (This soaking can be eliminated, but it shortens the cooking time and improves the final product.)
2. Drain the potatoes, dry them on a towel, then put them in a bowl or ziplock bag. Drizzle them with the oil and sprinkle with the salt and pepper, as desired. Toss to coat evenly.
3. Place the potatoes evenly on a nonstick shallow baking pan.
4. Bake at 425°F (220°C) for 15 minutes. Turn the potatoes over, sprinkle with the optional seasonings, as desired, and continue baking for another 10 to 15 minutes. Serve immediately. Be careful; the potatoes will be very hot!

Calories per potato:	260
Carbohydrates	52 grams
Protein	4
Fat	4

Chapter 8

Water and Sports Drinks

Today's marathoners know that preventing dehydration is an important part of their training and racing program. But that wasn't always the case. For example, in 1953, running regulations stated that marathoners could take water only after 9.3 miles. This contrasts to 2006, when most marathons provide water stations every one or two miles along their courses.

While dehydration is the main concern for marathoners, drinking *too much* water has created medical problems in a few overzealous drinkers. So what's the right balance of water and exercise? The American College of Sports Medicine recommends that you drink 4 to 8 ounces of fluid every 15 to 20 minutes of hard running. The Association of International Marathon Directors recommends you drink according to thirst. Thirst is a clear signal your body needs fluids. In either case, you should try to drink enough to match your sweat losses, but not over-hydrate. While dehydration is the far more common concern than overhydration, all athletes can avoid either problem by drinking according to their sweat rate.

To determine how much you should drink during exercise, weigh yourself (without clothes) before and after an hour of training. If you have lost one pound (16 ounces; 450 ml) in one hour, you've lost one pint (16 ounces; 450 ml) of sweat and should plan to drink accordingly during the next exercise session—at least 8 ounces (225 ml) every half-hour. You may need to weigh yourself at different seasons to determine if your sweat losses in winter are less than in summer. All marathoners in all climates in all seasons should make the effort to know their sweat rate. This includes those who:
- race in the summer heat
- overdress for a winter training run
- sweat hard when working out on the health club's treadmill

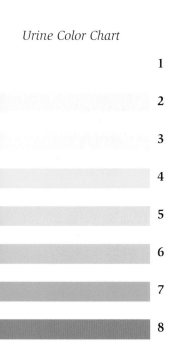

Urine Color Chart

1

2

3

4

5

6

7

8

Strive to lose no more than 2 percent of your body weight per exercise session. That is, if you weigh 150 pounds (68 kg), try not to lose more than 3 pounds (1.5 kg) of sweat during a workout. Practice drinking fluids on the run during training, so on marathon day you'll be familiar with the skills involved in drinking during exercise, as well as your body's capacity for fluids. If you plan to drink anything other than water during the marathon (e.g., a sports drink), be sure that you have tried it during training, as well.

You can tell if you are well hydrated by monitoring your urine:
- You should urinate frequently (every 2 to 4 hours) throughout the day.
- The urine should be clear and of significant quantity.
- Your morning urine should not be dark and concentrated.

This urine color chart (courtesy of Dr. Lawrence Armstrong) can quickly help you determine if you have been consuming enough fluids to stay well hydrated. If your urine is darker than 3, drink more! Lack of water slows you down and, in extreme cases, can contribute to medical problems. If you replace fluid losses poorly during training and are chronically dehydrated, you'll tend to experience needless fatigue and lethargy. Don't let that happen!

Sports Drinks

Although water is an adequate fluid replacement during short runs and walks (less than an hour), sports drinks are helpful during training sessions that last longer than 60 to 90 minutes. You'll perform better and feel better if you drink more than just plain water. Sports drinks provide:

In the summer, before my long runs, I drive along the course and hide water bottles in the shrubs and behind telephone poles. Most of the time, the water is there when I run by and need a drink.

Amy Singer, Seattle, WA

- small amounts of *carbohydrates* to fuel your mind and muscles
- *sodium* to enhance water absorption and retention
- *water* to replace sweat losses

With the multitude of sports drinks on the market, it is easy to feel confused about what's best to drink and to wonder if some are better than the others. The bottom line is you should choose the drink that you prefer; there are no significant advantages to one over the other.

The beverage perfect for all marathoners has yet to be designed. In the quest for developing the ideal sports beverage, scientists have observed enormous individual differences among people's stomach function during exercise. This helps explain why some people choose plain water, others seek out a particular brand of sports drink, and some prefer to make their own concoction. The most important point is to *drink enough*. Any fluid, be it water or sports drink, is better than no fluid During extended exercise.

If you prefer to abstain from sports drinks, the alternate way to consume adequate water and carbs is to have a pre-exercise snack and consume plain water plus jelly beans, gels, energy bars and other sources of carbs during the long run. See Chapter 10 for more information about Foods and Fluids during Long Walks and Runs.

I've solved the problem of getting sticky from sports drinks that splash all over me when I'm running in a race: I cut a straw in half and tuck it under my watchband. I then use the straw to drink from the cup while I'm running. I'm sure I end up drinking more fluids. The trick is to not drop the straw!

Bill Franks,
Sanbornton, NH

Sodium Replacement

When you sweat, you lose sodium, an electrolyte (electrically charged particle) that helps maintain proper water balance in your tissues. Most runners

Comparing Common Fluid Replacements

Beverage (8 oz)	Calories	Sodium (mg)	Potassium (mg)
Propel	10	35	0
Gatorade	50	110	30
Gatorade Endurance	50	200	90
PowerAde	70	55	30
Cola	100	5	0
Beer	100	12	60
Orange juice	110	2	475
Cranapple juice	175	5	70
Fruit yogurt	250	150	465
Possible losses in 2 hours	1,000	1,000	180

don't have to worry about replacing sodium during exercise because the losses are generally too small to cause a deficit that will hurt performance and/or health. But, if you will be exercising for more than four hours, sodium loss can become problematic, particularly if you are drinking only water during that time. Marathoners who drink excessive water dilute the sodium outside the cells; this causes too much water to seep into cells and the cells swell—including the cells in the brain. Symptoms that progressively appear include feeling weak, groggy, nauseous, incoherence, and ultimately stumbling, seizures, coma, or death.

Your best bet during extended exercise is to choose sports drinks *and* foods that contain sodium. The standard sports drink alone does not protect against hyponatremia because a sports drink offers far more water than sodium. The typical sports drink may have only 1/5th the concentration of normal blood serum. The sodium is added primarily to increase the absorption rate of the water into your body, not to replace the sodium lost in sweat.

Salt: Shake It or Leave It?

The rule of thumb is to add extra salt to your diet if you have lost more than four to six pounds of sweat (3–4 percent of your body weight pre- to post-exercise). Salty sweaters (who end up with a crust of salt on their skin after a hard workout) and heavy sweaters (who lose more than 2 lbs of sweat per hour) should pay close attention to their sodium intake—particularly if you are not acclimatized to running in the heat. For example, if you are training in the winter for a marathon that happens to land on an exceptionally warm spring day, you might need extra sodium during the marathon. Some marathoners choose Gatorade's Endurance Formula; others eat pretzels, drink V-8 juice along the way, or carry salt packets (from a restaurant).

In general, most marathoners consume adequate sodium, even without adding salt to their food. For example, you get sodium via bread (150 mg/slice), cheese (220 mg/1oz/30 g), eggs (60 mg/egg), and yogurt (125 mg/8 oz/240 ml). Athletes who are extreme sweaters likely need more sodium, but generally consume more, particularly if they eat fast foods. Just two slices of cheese pizza (1,200 mg) or a Whopper (1,450 mg) can easily replace sodium losses; no sweat!

If you crave salt, you should eat it. Salt cravings signal that your body wants salt. If you hanker for some pretzels or salty foods after a long run, eat them. Soup is another popular recovery food after a cold-weather run; the broth provides warmth, water and salt.

How to Keep Your Cool

The following true-false quiz is designed to test your knowledge about fluid replacement and help you survive the heat in good health and with high energy.

Drinking cold water during running will cool you off.
True (but by a small margin). Although drinking cold water will cool you off slightly more than warmer water, the difference is small. That's because the water quickly warms to body temperature. The more important concern is quantity. Any fluid of any temperature is better than no fluid.

Soda is a poor choice during exercise because the carbon dioxide in the bubbles will slow you down.
False. Historically, athletes were always warned to "de-fizz" carbonated beverages taken during exercise, fearing that the carbonation would interfere with oxygen transport and would also hurt performance. Not the case. Studies comparing carbonated and non-carbonated soft drinks suggest bubbles will not hurt your performance nor result in stomach discomfort.

Don't bother to drink during a run that is shorter than an hour because the fluid has too little time to get into your system.
False. According to Larry Armstrong, exercise physiologist at the University of Connecticut, water can travel from the stomach to skin 9 to 18 minutes after drinking. This water is essential for dissipating the 15 to 20 times more heat you produce during exercise as compared to that produced while you are at rest. Your safest bet is to try to match sweat losses with an equal volume of fluid during exercise.

Beer is an appropriate recovery fluid.
False. Although beer is a popular post-exercise recovery drink, its alcohol content has both a dehydrating and depressant effect. If you drink beer on an empty stomach (as commonly happens post-race), you can quickly negate the pleasurable "natural high" that you would otherwise enjoy. Wise beer-drinkers first have 1 to 2 glasses of water and eat some carbohydrate-rich foods (e.g., pretzels, pizza, crackers) and then they enjoy a beer or two in moderation.

Homemade Sports Drink

The main ingredients in commercial fluid replacers are:

Sugar: Sports drinks are 5 to 7 percent sugar; they contain about 12 grams of carbohydrates (50 calories) per 8 ounces. This is equal to 3 teaspoons (8 g) of sugar per cup.

Sodium: Sports drinks contain 50 to 110 milligrams of sodium per 8 ounces; this is equal to 1/8 teaspoon or 1 pinch of salt per cup.

This recipe comes close enough. Give it a try if you want a low-cost fluid replacer.

1/4 cup (30 g) sugar
1/4 teaspoon (1 g) salt
1/4 cup (60 ml) orange juice
3 1/2 cups (840 ml) cold water

1. In the bottom of a 1 quart (1 liter) bottle, dissolve the sugar in a little bit of hot water.
2. Add the salt and juice.
3. Add the cold water.
4. Quench that thirst!

YIELD: 1 quart or 4 8-oz servings (~ 1 liter; 4 240-ml)

Total calories: 200
Calories per serving: 50

Carbohydrates:	12 g
Protein:	0 g
Fat:	0 g
Sodium:	110 mg
Potassium:	30 mg

Chapter 9

Fueling Before You Exercise

One of the biggest mistakes made by novice marathoners (in particular, weight-conscious marathoners) is to train on empty. They think this will help them lose fat and run faster. Wrong! Just as your car works best with gas in its tank, your body works best when it has been appropriately fueled.

> **More marathons are won or lost in the portable toilets than they are on the roads.**
>
> Bill Rodgers,
> Boston, MA

But food can sometimes be a problem for people who fear food-related upset stomachs that interfere with exercise. Running and fast walking jostles your stomach and enhances your risk of intestinal distress. An estimated 25 to 30 percent of runners may experience abdominal cramps, diarrhea, and/or the need for pit stops during or immediately after running.

Pre-exercise food can offer you a competitive edge that contributes to greater stamina and endurance. If you have always abstained from eating a little bit of something before you exercise, I encourage you to try a light snack. You might be pleasantly surprised by the benefits that come from fueling up rather than running on empty.

Because eating ability and food preferences vary in relation to the type and intensity of exercise and the time of day, all marathoners should *practice* pre-exercise eating and remember that you are training your intestinal track as well as your heart, lungs and muscles. During training, you will learn through trial and error:
- what foods work best for your body
- when you should eat them
- what amounts are appropriate

Any of the following recommendations regarding pre-exercise eating should be pondered and experimented with during long runs, *not on marathon day.* You are an experiment of one; that is, only you can best determine what works best for you. And remember, food that you can tolerate on a normal training run may be intolerable during a marathon. Chalk that up to pre-event nervousness, not the food itself.

> **As a walker who became a runner, I have learned many things about my body. Initially, I couldn't eat before exercise or else I would get nauseated. Realizing I needed energy before heading out, I finally discovered that a glass of milk kick-starts me without ill effects. For longer distances, I bring dried fruit in my fanny pack.**
>
> Kim Holland,
> Maitland, FL

I emphasize *experiment during training* because here's what typically happens:

Marathoners read advertisements about special sports drinks, sports bars, supplements, or liquid meals. They are curious about trying these special products but because of their high price tag, they don't quite get around to buying them. Instead, they end up trying the free products provided by the sponsors on marathon day. In some instances, they discover (much to their dismay) that for them the unfamiliar food causes an upset stomach, heartburn, diarrhea, or cramps. If they had sampled these new products during training, they would be confident about whether or not to use the race-day samples.

What (and whether) you eat before exercise will vary according to:
- *The type of exercise.* Pre- run food may make you uncomfortable, but pre-walk or pre-bike food might not cause any problems.
- *How hard you will be working.* You may be able to eat within ten minutes of an easy training run, an hour before a marathon, but need to wait three hours before a track workout.
- *How nervous you are.* Nothing will settle well if your stomach is in knots.

The general rule of thumb is that the harder you exercise, the less likely you will want to eat, and the more likely you need to allow ample time between eating and exercising. Fast runners may feel nauseated at even the thought of pre-exercise food, but slow walkers will appreciate the added energy.

If you exercise at a pace that you can comfortably sustain for more than 30 minutes, you can likely both exercise and digest food at the same time. At a training pace, the blood flow to your stomach is 60 to 70 percent of normal—adequate to maintain normal digestion processes.

If you are doing intense sprint work, your stomach essentially shuts down and gets only about 20 percent of its normal blood flow. This slows the digestion process so that any pre-exercise food will jostle along for the ride, and possibly "talk back." It may feel uncomfortable and cause indigestion or heartburn.

Five Benefits of Pre-exercise Fueling

If you are in the experimental stage of developing your pre-exercise food plan for various intensity walks or runs, as well as for a marathon, the following information provides some helpful facts about the benefits of pre-exercise food. This information can help you on marathon day when the right combination of food and fluids will make or break your ability to complete the distance comfortably.

I've trained my body to thrive on pre-exercise food. From the beginning of my running career, I have always run with food in my stomach. I'd eat meals and snacks with my children so that I could enjoy family time with them, and then I'd run at night. I now have an iron stomach. I can eat and run—nothing bothers me.

Hal Gabriel,
Newton, MA

One year, the guy who was driving me to the marathon stopped for donuts, so I got some too. That was a mistake because I generally have only toast. The donuts landed like lead sinkers. I was in good shape for the marathon, but too many donuts did me in.

Gerry Beagan,
North Kingston, RI

1. *Pre-exercise food helps prevent low blood sugar.* Why suffer with light-headedness, needless fatigue, irritability, and inability to concentrate when you can prevent these symptoms of hypoglycemia?

The carbohydrates in your pre-exercise snack are important because they fuel not only your muscles but also your mind. Adequate carbohydrates help you think clearly because your brain fuels itself with glucose, the sugar in your blood that is derived from carbohydrates. As marathon legend Grete Waitz once commented, "Novice runners often fail to recognize how much mental energy and concentration is needed to run—especially to run a marathon."

Your blood sugar is maintained at a normal level by the release of sugar (glycogen) stored in your liver. If you have low blood sugar or a low liver glycogen (as happens overnight or in the afternoon if you fail to eat enough breakfast and lunch), your brain will be left unfed. You will feel tired and you won't be able to concentrate on the task at hand. You may feel like you've "hit the wall." Why suffer with needless fatigue when you can prevent (or at least, delay) fatigue by fueling yourself appropriately before you run?

If you run in the morning, you likely have to drag yourself through your workout if you haven't eaten anything between your 7:00 p.m. dinner and your 7:00 a.m. run.

Similarly, if you choose to eat nothing between the pre-marathon pasta party and the 10:45 a.m. start of the New York City Marathon or the noon start of the Boston Marathon, you'll begin the event depleted and may end up devastated. Your blood sugar levels will have dropped, particularly if you tossed and turned all night with pre-race anxiety. Some morning runners exercise with an empty stomach and report that they have plenty of energy. They have likely eaten a substantial dinner and/or done serious late-night snacking to bolster liver glycogen stores and reduce their need for a morning energizer. This is not bad or wrong, as long as this pattern works well for them. (But, in general, runners who do most of their eating at the end of the day tend to have more body fat than those who fuel well during the day. See Chapter 15, Weight Reduction for Marathoners, for more information on weight management.)

300-calorie Suggestions

According to research, you might be able to increase your stamina by as much as 18 percent if you take in 0.5 grams of carbohydrates per pound of body weight (or 1 gram per kilogram) per hour of endurance exercise. For example, if you weigh 150 pounds, you should target about 75 grams of carbohydrates (300 calories) per hour. This could be:

- six 8-ounce glasses of a sports drink (50 calories per 8 ounces)
- four cups of sports drink and a banana
- two cups of sports drink plus an energy bar (plus extra water)
- five fig cookies plus water

This is more calories than many marathoners voluntarily consume during long runs or walks. Hence, you need to practice programmed eating and drinking. Then, on marathon day, you will know:

- what and how much you can tolerate
- how you can comfortably carry the sports snacks

2. *Pre-exercise food helps settle the stomach, absorbs some of the gastric juices, and abates hunger feelings.* For many people, the stress associated with competition stimulates gastric secretions and contributes to an "acid stomach." Eating a small amount of food can help alleviate that problem.

The caloric density of a snack or meal affects the rate at which the food leaves your stomach. This explains why you can exercise comfortably soon after snacking on a few crackers or a piece of fruit but are better off waiting three or four hours after a heartier meal.

The general pre-exercise "rule of thumb" is to allow:

- 3–4 hours for a large meal to digest
- 2–3 hours for a smaller meal
- 1–2 hours for a blended or liquid meal
- less than an hour for a small snack, as tolerated

All the experimenting for marathon day should have been completed at least four weeks prior to the marathon. During these final four weeks, you should fine tune what you've learned to be sure that your body can handle your choice of foods and fluids.

John Correia,
San Diego, CA

Rather than eating a full pre-marathon breakfast, think about eating part of that breakfast the night before, prior to going to bed. (Experiment with this prior to long training runs.) This allows ample time for the food to digest and helps maintain a normal blood glucose level. You can then eat the second half of the breakfast when you get up at 5:00 a.m. for an 8:00 a.m. marathon start.

3. *Pre-exercise food fuels the muscles.* The food you eat even an hour before you exercise is digested into glucose and burned for energy. For example, one study showed that runners who ate 400 calories of sugar three hours before an easy four-hour run burned about 70 percent of the sugar. Without question, pre-run food that is well tolerated provides an energy boost that can enhance your stamina.

If you have trouble with solid foods such as a bagel, you might want to experiment with liquids, such as a fruit smoothie or a canned liquid meal such as Boost. One research study showed that a 450-calorie meal of steak, peas, and buttered bread took six hours to leave the stomach, whereas a blenderized variation of the same meal emptied from the stomach in four hours.

In general, carbohydrates are digested more easily than fatty foods. Low-fat foods and meals (such as those listed in the sidebar, High Carbohydrate Meal Suggestions, p. 87) tend to digest easily and settle well. In comparison, high-fat-bacon-and-fried-egg breakfasts, greasy hamburgers, tuna subs loaded with mayonnaise, and grilled cheese sandwiches have been known to settle heavily and feel uncomfortable. Too much fat slows digestion, so the meal lingers longer in the stomach and may contribute to a weighed-down feeling.

A little fat, however, such as in a slice of low-fat cheese on toast, a teaspoon of peanut butter on a bagel, or the fat in some brands of sports bars, can be appropriate. It provides both sustained energy and satiety during long runs.

Note that some marathoners can break all the sports nutrition rules and still do well even with very high-fat foods. After all, steak and eggs was the pre-marathon breakfast of champions for many years!

Pre-exercise Meals

To be sufficiently fueled for long training runs and walks, hard track workouts, shorter races, or the marathon, eat according to this schedule. Always drink additional fluids with and between meals to ensure complete hydration. If you are overly nervous, stressed, or have a sensitive stomach prior to the event, you may have to abstain from food on the day of competition and make a special effort to eat extra food the day before.

Morning events:

Day before: Minimal exercise
                        Eat a hearty, carbohydrate-based lunch,
                        dinner, and bedtime snack.

Race morning: Eat a light snack/breakfast to abate hunger feelings, and replenish liver glycogen stores.

Example:

Lunch: Turkey sub, pretzels, cranberry juice
Dinner: Spaghetti, with tomato sauce (and a little meat), bread, frozen yogurt
Bedtime: Bagel with light cream cheese and jam, orange juice
Breakfast: Oatmeal, banana

Afternoon events:

Day before: Minimal exercise
                        Eat a hearty carbohydrate-based dinner.

Race day: Eat a hearty carbohydrate-based breakfast and a light lunch.

Example:

Dinner: Small chicken breast, lots of rice, winter squash, rolls, fig bars, apple cider
Breakfast: Pancakes, syrup, melon, pineapple juice
Lunch: Turkey sandwich and/or chicken noodle soup, crackers

Evening events:

Day before: Minimal exercise
                        Eat carbohydrate-based meals.

Race day: Eat a hearty carbohydrate-based breakfast and lunch, followed by a light snack 1 to 3 hours prior to the event.

Example:

Breakfast: Grapenuts, (canned) peaches, low-fat milk, English muffin, honey, orange juice
Lunch: Big bagel with peanut butter, jelly, animal crackers, cranapple juice
Snack: Energy bar, yogurt, banana as desired

High-Carbohydrate Meal Suggestions

Some high-carbohydrate meal suggestions for both training and pre-marathon include tried-and-true foods such as:

Breakfast: Cold cereals, oatmeal and other hot cereals, bagels, English muffins, pancakes, french toast with syrup, jam, honey, fruit, juice

Lunch: Sandwiches (with the bread being the "meat " of the sandwich), fruit, thick-crust pizza, hearty broth-based soups with noodles or rice

Dinner: Pasta, potato, or rice entrées; veggies, breads, juice, fruit

Snacks: Flavored yogurt, pretzels, crackers, fig bars, frozen yogurt, dry cereal, leftover pasta, zwieback, energy bars, simple biscuit-type cookies, animal crackers, canned and fresh fruits, juice

4. *Pre-exercise beverages can provide fluids (to fully hydrate your body), as well as provide additional carbohydrates.* By tanking up on diluted juice or sports drinks before you exercise, you can help prevent dehydration, as well as boost your carbohydrate and energy intake. Whereas you are unlikely to starve during the marathon, you may become seriously injured due to dehydration. The best pre-exercise fluid choices include water, sports drinks, diluted juices and even coffeee or tea, if you want a caffeine boost and typically consume caffeinated beverages.

You should drink plenty of fluids not only before marathons and other races but also every day during training, in both hot and cold weather. You can confirm that you've had enough to drink by frequent urination and clear-colored urine. If your urine is dark and concentrated, you need more fluids. Refer to Chapter 8 for more information on hydration.

5. *Pre-exercise food can pacify your mind with the knowledge that your body is well fueled.* Before a long training run or walk, and particularly before a marathon, you don't want to waste any energy wondering if you've eaten enough. Appropriate eating can resolve that concern!

Pre-exercise food has great psychological value. If you firmly believe that a specific food or meal will enhance your performance, then it probably will. Your mind has a powerful effect on your body's ability to perform at its best. If you do have a "magic food" that assures athletic excellence, you should take special care to be sure this food or meal is available prior to the race.

Summary

Whether you are a walker or a runner, pre-exercise food will help you better enjoy your marathon training program. Just as you put gas in your car before you take it for a drive, you should put 100 to 300 calories of carbohydrate-rich food in your body before you exercise. You need to train your intestinal track to tolerate this fuel, just as you are training your heart, lungs and muscles to go the distance. Granted, each marathoner is an experiment of one, and some marathoners can tolerate food better than others; that's why you need to experiment during training to determine what pre-exercise menu works best for you.

Sugar and Spice Trail Mix

This crunchy munchie is a welcome snack for hungry marathoners who want something that's sweet, but not too sweet. Store the trail mix in individual portions in zip-lock bags, and keep it handy for a mid-afternoon energizer before you exercise, or for a travel-snack when you are on the road.

This recipe, as well as many other healthful yet tasty recipes, can be found on the American Heart Associations Website, *www. deliciousdecisions.org.*

3 cups (170 g) Oat Squares cereal
3 cups (170 g) mini-pretzels, salted or salt-free, as desired
2 tablespoons (30 g) tub margarine, melted
1 tablespoon (10 g) packed brown sugar
1/2 teaspoon (2.5 g) cinnamon
1 cup (140 g) dried fruit bits or raisins

1. Preheat oven to 325°F (160°C).
2. In a large plastic zip-lock bag or plastic container with a cover, combine the oat squares and pretzels.
3. In a small bowl, stir together the melted maragarine, brown sugar and cinnamon. Pour over the cereal mixture.
4. Seal the bag or container and shake gently until the mixture is well coated. Transfer to a baking sheet.
5. Bake, uncovered, for 15 to 20 minutes, stirring once or twice.
6. Let cool, then add the dried fruit.
7. Store in an airtight container or smaller single-serving baggies.

Yield: 10 servings (about 2/3 cup)
Total calories: 2,000
Calories per serving: 200

Carbohydrates: 40 g
Protein: 5 g
Fat: 2 g

Reprinted with permission from the American Heart Association and *Nancy Clark's Sports Nutrition Guidebook, Third Edition*, Human Kinetics, 2003.

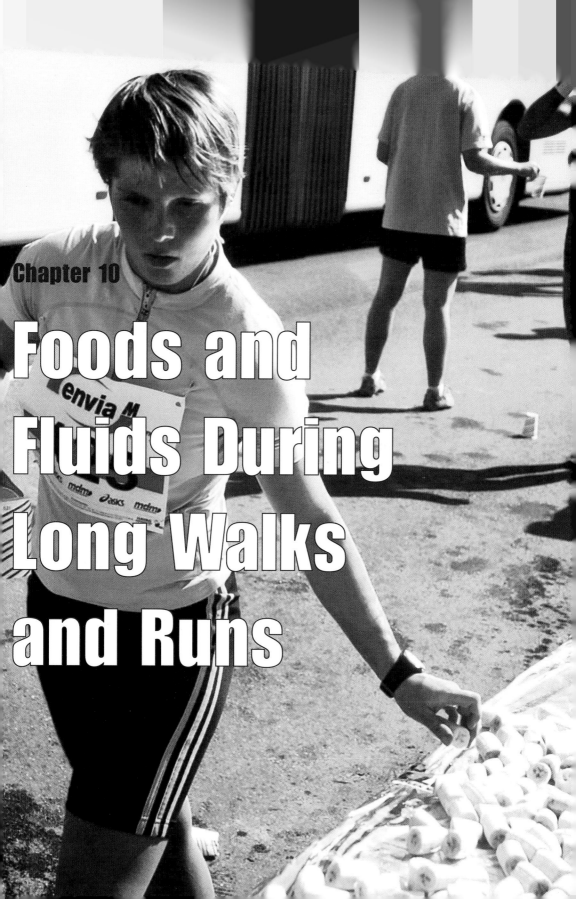

Chapter 10

Foods and Fluids During Long Walks and Runs

Whether you are hoping to complete the marathon in three hours or six hours, the single most important nutrition tip is to learn *during* training sessions how to eat for the marathon. Learn to eat early and often, and learn what types of foods and fluids your body can tolerate. As I've mentioned before, your training runs and walks are to train not only your heart, lungs and muscles, but also your intestinal tract so you can keep yourself well fueled and hydrated, and so you can delay fatigue and prevent dehydration without discomfort or undesired pit stops.

As an endurance athlete, your goals are to:
1) drink enough fluid to prevent dehydration (and not become overhydrated) and
2) consume enough carbs to prevent hypoglycemia (low blood sugar).
You can succeed at meeting these goals by drinking carbohydrate-containing fluids (such as a sports drink) or by combining water with solid foods (water + energy bar). Although you'll rarely see elite runners consuming more than a sports drink, slower marathoners can do well with a variety of fluids and foods that they have tested during training.

Beginning walkers, in particular, could carry with them a veritable picnic basket – energy bars, trail mix, sports drinks, even sandwiches and fruit – for any distance over 90 minutes. I've seen too many walkers dragging on the course, drained of energy and dehydrated. Many are walking for over 8 hours, and they would have normally eaten at least two meals during that time frame.

Creating a Fueling Plan

During training and marathons, be sure to drink every 15 to 20 minutes. Remember, you want to *prevent* dehydration. Don't let yourself get too thirsty. By drinking on a schedule – let's say, a target of about 4-8 ounces (120-240 ml), that's 4-8 gulps of water or sports drink every 15 to 20 minutes – you can minimize dehydration, maximize your performance, and reduce your recovery time.

As was discussed in Chapter 8, learning your sweat rate helps you determine how much to drink—particularly if you sweat heavily. Be certain you make the effort to weigh yourself before and after a one-hour run so you'll know how much sweat you lose (and need to replace); one pound sweat = one pound of water lost (16 ounces; 480 g).

Start drinking within a half-hour to prevent dehydration; once you are dehydrated, you won't catch up. Losing only 2 percent of your body weight (3 pounds for a 150-pound person; 1.4 kg. for a 70 kg person) from sweating hurts your performance and upsets your ability to regulate your body temperature. (Refer to Chapter 8 for more details.) To keep hydrated:
- If you are training with a group, take advantage of the water stations your coach has set up along the route.
- If you are in a race, know in advance the location of each water station. If there is a water station every mile, you might want to drink at every other station (every 15 to 20 minutes) or according to thirst.
- If you are training by yourself, set up your own water stops. This means planning a route that includes adequate water fountains, or driving the route before your run/walk and placing bottles filled with water or sports drinks in strategic locations.

- Take fluids with you. Some marathoners prefer to run with a Camelback (water bladder that straps to the back) or other portable water system.

Yes, you want to drink according to a schedule, but also pay attention to thirst. Don't force fluids. Drinking too much fluid to the point you feel the excess water sloshing around in your stomach also causes problems—nausea, if not hyponatremia (low blood sodium). The immediate solution is to stop drinking for a while. The long-term solution is to practice drinking during training, so your body can adapt to the appropriate fluid intake.

You will feel happier and more energetic if you can replace not only water but also carbohydrates while running or walking. These carbohydrates help to maintain a normal blood sugar level, as well as provide a source of energy for muscles. Then, during the marathon, when you come to the 18- or 20-mile mark, you can breeze right though it to the finish—and avoid hitting "the wall."

Fanny packs or running shorts with multiple pockets are a good way to carry your snacks. Some marathoners set the timer on their watch to go off every 30 to 45 minutes to ensure they'll eat on a schedule. You might also want to have friends meet you at designated areas along the course. Also check the marathon's website to find out what snacks they will offer along the route. But always carry some back-up fuel with you in case you miss seeing the friends or the snack table runs out of gels or has only the yucky flavor left.

Whatever you do, think ahead and make a clear plan before marathon day. You must also be flexible. Who knows what will happen when your body is pushed to the limit. Even tried-and-true favorites can become unpalatable.

Popular Snacks During a Long Run

A plethora of commercial sports snacks are available for marathoners, yet "real foods" can work just as well. Experiment with a variety of textures (soft, hard, dry, moist) and flavors (sweet, sour, salty), knowing that tastes change over the course of 26.2 miles.

Solids:
Dried figs
Energy bar
Bagel
Tootsie Rolls
Hard candies
Mini chocolate bars
Gummy candies
Sports beans
Vanilla cookies
Pretzels
Banana

Liquids:
Diluted, defizzed cola
Sports drinks
Iced tea with honey
Diluted juice
Iced coffee with sugar
Honey sticks
Gels
Broth (for salt)
Meal-in-a-can
(Boost, Ensure)
Go-Gurt
(squeeze-pack yogurt)
Water
(with solid food)

> During a marathon, I prefer Swedish fish (gummy candy) over the gels because, as some runners know, gels sometimes send runners to the porta-potties during the race. Swedish fish give me an immediate sugar-fix, take the edge off the light-headed feeling, and don't leave me feeling sick afterwards. You can even bite down on this candy and it will stay in your teeth to keep the glucose coming. Perhaps this is not so great for your teeth, but it works for me.

Valerie Watson, OH

Commercial Sports Foods

Ever feel confused by the plethora of commercial sports foods from which to choose? A multitude of businesses have jumped on the bandwagon to create products that appeal to a variety of athletes, from those with special dietary requests (gluten-free, vegan) to those who are just plain hungry and want a "politically correct" candy bar (Marathon Bar). When it comes to what to buy, there is no "best choice"; you simply need to experiment to determine what products satisfy your taste buds and settle well. Most of the sports products claim to be easy to digest, but you will have to determine that for yourself!

Today's $2-billion-plus sports fuel industry is indeed booming; busy athletes enjoy the convenience, taste and ease of using designer sports foods. While these commercial sports foods tend to be more about convenience than necessity, they can make fueling easier for busy marathoners. Just keep in mind "real food" (dried figs, gummy bears, chocolate milk) can often do the same job at a lower price. After all, athletes managed to survive and perform well for years prior to the 1970s (when Gatorade grew in popularity), 1980s (when PowerBar was introduced), and 1990s (when gels entered the sports scene). Certainly, there is a time and place for all of these products. Just be sure you maintain a foundation of wholesome foods in the midst of the manufactured choices. There should be a few apple cores and banana peels along with the wrapper litter.

Below is a comprehensive (but unlikely complete) list of various types of sports fuels and foods. Perhaps it will help you untangle the jungle of choices. Don't be swayed by a product's name; it might be more powerful than the sports food itself.

SPORTS DRINKS

With sodium (and perhaps other electrolytes):
Gatorade, Edge Energy, Hydro-Boom!, GU2O, CytoMax, Clif Shot Electrolyte, Motor Tabs , Perpetuem

All-natural without dye/food coloring:
First Endurance EFS, Clif Shot Electrolyte Drink, Hammer Nutrition HEED, Recharge

Extra sodium (good idea if you plan to exercise for >2 hours in the heat):
Gatorade Endurance, PowerBar Endurance, E-Fuel, First Endurance EFS, Clif Shot Electrolyte Drink, E-Load, Hydro Pro Cooler

Added "buffers": Cytomax, Perpetuem, Revenge Sport

Extra carbs: Carbo-Pro

Added protein (May reduce post-exercise muscle soreness):
Amino Vital, Perpetuem, Accelerade, Revenge Pro

Sports drinks for dieters (i.e., lower calorie):
PowerAde Option, Ultima Replenisher, Xtra LowOz, Propel, Nuun

GELS
(Test with these during training. They can taste very sweet and are common contributors to diarrhea.)
Gu, Carb-BOOM!, Clif Shot, Honey Stinger (all natural), Hammer Gel

Extra sodium: PowerBar Gel, Crank Sports e-Gel, Pro Boom

Added protein: Accel Gel, Endless edge, Pro Boom

Added caffeine: GU Espresso Love, Clif Shot Mocha, Cola and Strawberry; Carb-BOOM Chocolate Cherry, Hammer Gel Espresso, PowerBar Gel Double Latte, Tangerine, Chocolate, Green Apple and Strawberry-banana; Honey Stinger Ginsting and Strawberry

Added extras: EAS Energy Gel (taurine)

ENDURANCE FOOD
Jelly Belly Sports Beans (a jelly bean with sodium). Clif Shot Bloks (a soft gummi candy in a block), Sharkies (organic fruit chew), SPIZ ("liquid food")

RECOVERY DRINKS *(Carbs with a little protein)*
Amino Vital, First Endurance E3, EAS Endurathon, Perpetuem, PowerBar Recovery Drinks, Recoverite, Go Energy Drink, Endurox R4, Gatorade Nutrition Shake, Hormel's Great Shake, GNC's Distance, Clif Shot Recovery Drink. First Endurance Ultragen

ENERGY DRINKS (Concentrated sugar, often with added caffeine)
Red Bull, Rock Star, Monster, Rebound-fx, Full Throttle

ENERGY BARS (should be eaten for extra energy, not for a meal replacement)
All natural/organic (have no added vitamins or minerals):
Clif Bar, Peak Energy, Perfect 10, Clif Nectar, Clif Mojo, Lara Bar, Optimum, TrailMix HoneyBar, Odwalla Bar, PowerBar Nut Naturals, Honey Stinger Bars, Kashi Bars

Granola-type bars: PowerBar Harvest, Nature Valley Granola Bar, Quaker Chewy Bars, Nutri-Grain Bar, Fig Newtons

Women's bars (fewer calories; soy, calcium, iron and folic acid):
PowerBar Pria, Amino Vital Fit, Luna Bar, Balance Oasis

40-30-30 Bars: Balance Bar, ZonePerfect

Kosher: Pure Fit, Lara Bar, Extend Bar

Dairy-free: Clif Nectar, Pure Fit, Perfect 10, Lara Bar, Clif Builder's Bar

Gluten-free: Perfect 10, Elev8Me, Hammer Bar, Clif Nectar, EnvirKids Rice Cereal Bar; Omega Smart Bars, Odwalla Bar, Clif Builder's Bar, Extend Bar

Fructose-free: JayBar

Vegan: Pure Fit, Lara Bar, Hammer Bar, Vega Whole Food Raw Energy Bar, Clif Builder's Bar, Perfect 10

Low fiber: Balance Bar

Bars with caffeine: Peak Energy Plus

Vitamin & protein-pumped candy bar: Marathon Bar, Detour Bar

Recovery bar (4:1 carb:pro ratio): PowerBar Performance

PROTEIN BARS (Your choice of soy, whey, egg, or blended protein source) PowerBar ProteinPlus, EAS Myoplex Delux, High 5 Protein Bar, Maximuscle Promax Meal, USN Pure Protein, Atkins Advantage, Tri-O-Plex, Clif Builder's Bar, Detour Bar, Honey Stinger Protein Bar

MEAL REPLACEMENT BARS (offers 10-15 g protein, fiber, some fat, vitamins, minerals-but not really enough calories for a whole meal) Kashi Go Lean Bar, Balance Satisfaction, MetRx Mr. Big, MET-Rx Big 100 Colossal

Fuel Suggestions

Whereas the fastest runners are able to do well with just carbohydrate-containing fluids, slower runners and walkers, who are going to be on the marathon course longer, will likely do better with not only fluids but also solids that provide more calories and also a flavor change. (Just how many hours in a row can you consume sports drinks and gels without getting "sugared-out"?) There is no magic to the special sports foods (e.g., gels, sports beans, energy bars) that are available at your local running store. These engineered foods are simply pre-wrapped and convenient ... use them if you prefer, but also know you could save money by eating sugar cookies and twizzlers.

The carbs you consume during the marathon will also keep you in good spirits. Some runners become moody, irritable, and irrational towards the end of a marathon. Running partners can become either the best of friends or the worst of enemies.

Undesired Pit Stops

Many marathoners fear that fluids or foods taken during the event will cause diarrhea. Diarrhea commonly occurs in novice runners, whose intestinal tracts are not fully adjusted to the jostling of 26.2 miles. With experience, the problem tends to abate, but some experienced runners learn to carry toilet paper with them. If you fear diarrhea attacks, experiment during training with dietary changes to see if eating less fiber (such as bran cereals and lots of whole grains, fruits and vegetables) can reduce the problem. Or try less milk (switch to lactose-free milk products). Some athletes simply need to abstain from food for three or four hours pre-event.

Diarrhea is also common among marathoners who lose more than 4 percent of their body weight during the race (6 pounds for a 150-pound person; 3 kg/70 kg). Hence, the fluids you drink may actually help prevent diarrhea, not cause it. I once talked to a runner who tried to abstain from drinking anything—even water—during a marathon in fear it would upset his stomach. He held off as long as he could without fluids. Then when he did succumb, he got diarrhea. Although he blamed the diarrhea on the drink, I tend to think the lack of prior fluid intake was the bigger problem.

For the walkers and slower runners who will be out for 6 or more hours, I recommend peanut-butter-and-honey sandwiches, just like mom made when you were a kid. Make them up the night before so the bread really soaks up the honey.

Earl Fenstermacher,
Seattle, WA

Because I am a slow runner, I would typically get hungry during a long run and my energy level would plummet. I would try eating yet-another sweet sports bar, which is full of carbohydrates, but it did very little to help; I had already had my fill of carbs. I realized that my body was craving something more solid; so I switched to a sports bar that has more protein. That has made all the difference.

Brenda Van Oosten,
Brecksville, OH

Summary

Preventing dehydration and low blood sugar is crucial to a successful marathon. The fluids and foods that you consume during your long walks or runs should be an extension of your carbohydrate-rich daily training diet. Because each marathoner has individual tolerances and preferences, you want to learn by trial and error during training, what foods and fluids settle best and contribute to top competitive performance. Don't ruin months of physical training—and your marathon—with poor nutrition training.

Honey Crisp Energy Bar

This energy bar is easy to make and yummy to eat! The more nuts and fruits you add to this recipe, the more wholesome it becomes.

1/4 cup (120 ml) canola oil
1/4 cup (120 ml) honey
5 oz (1/2 of a 10-oz bag; 140 g) marshmallows
2 cups uncooked oatmeal
2 cups toasted rice cereal, such as Rice Crispies
1/2 tsp salt, as desired

Optional: 1 cup chopped almonds or other nuts, 1 cup dried fruit of your choice (raisins, craisins, chopped apricots, dried blueberries, dried cherries, etc.)

- In a large saucepan, combine the oil, honey and marshmallows and heat over medium-low heat. Stir constantly until the marshmallows are melted.
- Mix in the oats and toasted rice cereal and other optional ingredients, as desired. Mix well.
- Pour into a greased 8" x 8" (20 x 20cm) pan. Using greased hands or spatula, spread the mixture evenly into the pan.
- When the mixture has cooled, cut it into 8 bars or squares.

Total calories (without any optional ingredients): 2,100
10 servings

Per serving:
Calories: 210
Carbohydrates: 35 g
Proteins: 2 g
Fat: 7 g

Chapter 11

Recovering from Exhaustive Training

You haven't finished training until you have refueled! That's right; refueling after you walk or run is just as important as fueling up beforehand. So before you dash off to to a post-workout obligation (school, work, meeting, etc.), be sure to eat; eating anything is better than nothing, even if you have to gobble the food on the run! By refueling your muscles, you can better endure repeated days—and months—of hard workouts. You need to pay close attention to your recovery diet after your *hard* workouts. That is, on easy days, you have less muscle damage from which you are recovering, so immediate refueling is less critical (but never-the-less, a good habit to maintain). However, after long runs, speed workouts and hill workouts, you'll optimize recovery and reduce muscle soreness if you rapidly refuel.

Proper recovery diets are particularly important for marathoners who do double workouts (such as run in the morning, then lift weights in the afternoon) or for weekend warriors (who do their long run, then ski the rest of the day with their family). They need to rapidly refuel because they are exercising within six hours. They don't have time to waste; their muscles need fuel as soon as tolerable post-exercise to prepare for the soon-to-come second workout.

Perhaps you are wondering what you should eat to hasten recovery? Here are the answers to questions marathoners commonly ask about recovery foods.

What is the Best Recovery Food Plan?

During a hard workout, you damage your muscles with tiny injuries and deplete your muscles of glycogen. Hence, afterwards, you should optimize recovery by consuming a little protein to repair the muscle damage and carbs to refuel the depleted glycogen stores. You don't need to eat tons of food—about 200 to 400 calories (50 to 100 g; 0.5 to 0.75 g carb/lb; 1.0-1.5 g carb/kg) of carbohydrate-based foods along with about 10 grams of protein within an hour after hard exercise. Then repeat this dose every 1 to 2 hours for five or six hours. Most marathoners tend to naturally follow this pattern with repeated meals and snacks, assuming they are not "dieting' or "too busy" to eat.

Good carb + protein recovery choices include:
- fruit yogurt
- chocolate milk
- cereal with milk
- turkey on a bulkie roll
- chicken dinner with rice and vegetables
- spaghetti with meat sauce

If you are on the road, carry with you:
- trail mix (nuts and raisins)
- bagel with peanut butter
- Go-gurt (liquid yogurt)
- Energy bar with 3 to 4 times as many carbs as protein

Some marathoners like commercial recovery drinks, like Accelerade or Endurox. Just remember: these manufactured foods lack all the health-protective nutrients that you get in "real food," so be sure to balance them into an overall healthful diet.

What if I'm Not Hungry after a Run?

If you get hot and sweaty during a long run, you might not feel hungry right away. But sooner or later, when your body temperature returns to normal, you will get hungry and be ready to eat; after all, you burn about 1,000 calories or more during a 10 miler! The sooner you refuel, the sooner your muscles have the tools (protein and carbs) they need to recover— and the sooner you will feel better. So rather than "hold off" until you feel hungry, at least drink some fluids to quench your thirst—preferably chocolate milk (for carbs and protein). If not chocolate milk, then juices or sports drinks.

 When I come back from a long, hard training run, I'm generally exhausted and in need of some quick energy. I've been known to drink maple syrup right from the bottle. Tastes great!

Bill Rodgers,
Boston, MA

If even the thought of post-exercise food or fluids makes you nauseated, you likely had a very tough workout. After a 20 + mile training run or the marathon itself, many marathoners have no interest in putting anything in their stomachs! In such a case, try to drink a little ginger ale (or some beverage that appeals to you) to settle your stomach and give you a few carbs and some fluid. But the reality is, you will likely be taking a rest day the next day, so your muscles will have time to refuel and recover before your next workout. Rapid refueling is most important for runners who train twice in a day or do hard efforts day after day. Yet, rapid refueling does reduce muscle soreness, so for that reason alone, try to eat or drink as soon as tolerable. Any fuel is better than no fuel.

How Much Should I Drink?

You should replace fluid losses as soon as possible to help your body restore normal water balance. If you weighed yourself pre- and post-exercise, you'll know exactly how much you dehydrated, how much you need to drink to rehydrate—and how much more you should drink on future runs to prevent the deficit in the first place. That is, if you started your run at 130 pounds and ended at 128 pounds, you lost 2 pounds (32 ounces, 1 quart) of sweat. Rehydrate with at least 1 quart (2 lbs), if not 50% more. And during your next training session on that route, plan to drink an additional quart of fluid.

Throughout the day, keep a water bottle on your desk, in your car, or in your backpack, so you'll easily be able to drink enough to quench your thirst. Sometimes, you may not feel thirsty, but your body may need more fluids. You'll know that you are well hydrated when you need to urinate every 2 to 4 hours and have pale-colored urine. Refer to Chapter 8 for a urine color chart and more information.

 At the end of each long walk, I have found that I recover much more quickly if I sip on orange juice and eat at least half a banana.

Shelley Smith,
Highlands Ranch, CO

What Should I Drink?

Here are some popular fluid options and how to balance them into your sports diet:

- *Plain water.* Water provides only water but not the carbohydrates you need to replenish depleted muscle glycogen nor the protein you need to repair and build muscles. Consume carb-protein foods along with the water, such as a bagel with peanut butter, apple with cheese, or energy bar (with both carbs and protein). Snacking on some salty foods (baked chips, pretzels, pizza) along with the plain water (or any beverage, for that matter) provides sodium, which enhances fluid absorption and retention.
- *Soft drinks.* Colas, in particular, are popular recovery fluids. Granted, soft drinks lack nutritional value and are filled with empty calories, but they do offer both carbohydrates and fluids. Most colas also offer caffeine, which for some may provide welcome stimulation. Historically, marathoners have been told to avoid caffeine because of a supposed diuretic effect. Newer research indicates caffeine is not dehydrating and is unlikely to hinder recovery.
- *Juices.* Fruit and vegetable juices are always an excellent choice because they not only offer a rich supply of carbohydrates, but they also offer the vitamin C your body needs to optimize healing. Blend some orange juice with a banana and some yogurt, and you'll have a powerful recovery drink!
- *Sports drinks.* Commercial fluid replacers are designed to be used during exercise; they are diluted and easy to digest. They provide fewer recovery carbohydrates than juices or soft drinks. That is, 8 ounces of a commercial fluid replacer offers half the carbohydrates of 8 ounces of most juices. Sports drinks are a fair source of carbs, and a poor source of vitamins.
- *Commercial recovery drinks.* Some sports drinks (such as Endurox, Accelerade) come with a little protein added; those might be better than drinks with only carbs (Gatorade, PowerAde). These commercial beverages are convenient, but they offer nothing that cannot be found in standard foods. In fact, they offer less; they lack the nutritional power of a multitude of vitamins and phytochemicals found in wholesome foods. While there is a time and a place for convenience, in the long run, you'll be better off refueling yourself primarily with real foods that are "closer to the earth" than a commercial carb-protein-vitamin formula. I encourage my clients to enjoy fruit smoothies or chocolate milk.

Do I Need Extra Salt to Replace What I Lose in Sweat?

In most cases, marathoners can replace more than enough salt by eating standard foods after exercise. Both walkers and runners lose some sodium (a part of salt) in sweat but are unlikely to deplete their body stores, even during a marathon. As I mentioned in Chapter 8, during three hours of sweaty exercise, you might lose about 1,800 to 5,600 milligrams of sodium. Since the average 150-pound person's body contains about 97,000 milligrams of sodium, this 2 to 6 percent loss is relatively insignificant.

But there are exceptions to every rule. Some marathoners are sweating for 6 hours—and have twice that loss. Others are salty sweaters and end up with a crusty layer of salt on their body. If this sounds familiar, you'll likely crave salt. In such case, you should respond appropriately by eating salty foods, such as salted pretzels, soups, crackers and/or baked potatoes or other foods sprinkled with salt.

Athletes who may need extra salt include:
- slower marathoners who exercise continuously for more than four to six hours
- people who train in cold weather yet run a marathon in warm weather. This some-times happens, for example, with Boston Marathoners if they train throughout the winter but compete on what turns out to be an unusually warm spring day. It also happens with people who live in cold climates, like Minnesota, but run a marathon where the weather is hot, such as Hawaii.
- marathoners who drink only water (as opposed to a sodium-containing sports drink) during extended runs or walks.

Popular Recovery Foods

Your muscles are most receptive to replacing depleted glycogen stores immediately after exercise. By feeding them carbohydrates, preferably with a little bit of protein, you can optimize the recovery process. Don't get hung-up on the recommended 4 to 1 ratio of carbs to protein; just enjoy wholesome carb-based foods that will refuel depleted glycogen stores. Include a little protein to repair and build muscles, but do not emphasize the protein.

If you can't tolerate solid foods immediately following a hard run or marathon, simply drink carbohydrate-rich fluids and/or eat watery foods, building up to mini-meals or snacks. Target 60 to 90 grams of carbs every two hours or so.

Some popular choices include:

Fluids (8 oz; 240 ml):	Carb (g)	Protein (g)
Gatorade	14	–
Coke	26	–
Cranberry juice	43	–
Accelerade	14	3
Chocolate milk	26	8
Yogurt, flavored	40	10

Solids:		
Trail mix (raisins, granola, nuts)	40	10
PowerBar, chocolate	45	10
Cheerios w/ milk	50	12
Pasta, 2 cups + meat sauce	100	20

Do I Need Extra Protein?

While eating a little protein along with recovery carbohydrates is a smart choice, you do not need to "protein load" and eat a protein-based recovery diet. That is, do not choose a protein bar or protein shake for your recovery food unless it has three or four times more carbs than protein. (Read the food label to determine the carb and protein content of the product.)

My favorite recovery foods are a handful of salted, dry roasted peanuts and a stack of Fig Newtons.

Earl Fernstermacher,
Seattle, WA

At recovery meals, if you fill up on a cheese omlet, steak, or chicken caesar salad, you'll miss out on the carbohydrate-rich bagel, potato and bread that you need to refuel depleted glycogen stores. In general, most marathoners can meet their protein needs with:

- a serving of protein-rich food at two meals a day (such as turkey on sandwich at lunch and lean hamburger in spaghetti sauce at dinner) plus
- a serving of dairy food at each meal (such as low-fat milk on cereal, a yogurt at lunch, and (low-fat) cheese with crackers before dinner; soy alternatives are fine). Refer to Chapter 6 for more information.

Many marathoners report craving protein after hard exercise. If that's the case for you, eat the burger, but be sure to also eat the roll and other carbohydrate-rich foods as an accompaniment. This balance will help you rebuild and refuel, as well as enjoy the recovery process.

Recovering from the Marathon

Some runners and walkers are all smiles after crossing the finish line. Others feel nauseous, achey, and horrid. Hopefully, you will have consumed the optimal combination of water, carbs and sodium during the marathon to put you into the "exhilarated" category. But if you are feeling nauseous, try sipping on ginger ale or cola. Some salty, brothy chicken noodle soup might taste good, as might a few saltines or pretzels. The sooner you can get fluids, carbs and sodium into your system, the better you will start to feel.

However you feel, you can be proud of your accomplishment. Many marathoners participate in a post-marathon celebration with yummy foods. Because you'll have plenty of time after the marathon to replace depleted glycogen stores, you can be less strict with choosing recovery carbohydrates (as discussed at the beginning of this chapter) and go with what you want and perhaps crave. For some, that's potato chips, for others it's a thick steak.

Yes, you do want to continue to eat:

- plenty of post-marathon recovery carbohydrates to refuel your muscles
- adequate protein (to help with healing damaged muscles)
- salty foods to replace electrolyte losses
- nutrient-dense fruits and vegetables to optimize health

But you need not be obsessive with your recovery diet because you will not be demanding much from your muscles for a while.

If you choose to celebrate with beer, wine, or champagne, be sure to eat something (anything!) first so that you are not drinking alcohol on an empty stomach, and also drink some juice or soft drinks for fluids and carbohydrates.

Surprisingly, you might even have energy to enjoy the post-marathon dance party if you allow yourself time to rest and eat well (as opposed to rush off to the airport to fly home). A nice massage and a gentle swim or bike ride to loosen stiff

As I mentioned in Chapter 8, during three hours of sweaty exercise, you might lose about 1,800 to 5,600 milligrams of sodium. Since the average 150-pound person's body contains about 97,000 milligrams of sodium, this 2 to 6 percent loss is relatively insignificant.

But there are exceptions to every rule. Some marathoners are sweating for 6 hours—and have twice that loss. Others are salty sweaters and end up with a crusty layer of salt on their body. If this sounds familiar, you'll likely crave salt. In such case, you should respond appropriately by eating salty foods, such as salted pretzels, soups, crackers and/or baked potatoes or other foods sprinkled with salt.

Power Pancakes

These pancakes are a yummy recovery breakfast with a good balance of carbs + protein. Although cottage cheese may sound like an unusual ingredient, you won't even notice it. Rather, it contributes to a very satisfying meal. The wheat germ adds vitamin E, B-vitamins and fiber.

1/2 cup (110 g) cottage cheese, preferably low-fat
1/2 cup (30 g) wheat germ
2 to 4 tablespoons (10 to 20 g) firmly packed brown sugar or honey
1 egg or substitute
1 to 2 tablespoons (15 to 30 g) oil, preferably canola
1 cup (240 ml) milk, preferably low-fat
1 teaspoon (5 g) vanilla extract
1 teaspoon (5 g) baking powder
1/2 teaspoon (2.5 g) baking soda
1 cup (120 g) flour, preferably half white, half whole wheat

Optional
1/2 teaspoon (2.5 g) cinnamon or 1/4 teaspoon (1 g) nutmeg
1. In a medium bowl, beat together the cottage cheese, wheat germ, brown sugar, egg and oil.
2. Beat in the milk and vanilla, then the baking powder and soda. Gently stir in the flour.
3. For each pancake, pour about 1/4 cup (60 ml) of batter onto a hot griddle. Cook pancakes until the edges are done and bubbles form on the top. Turn and cook until golden.
4. Serve plain or with maple syrup, applesauce with cinnamon, or yogurt.

Yield: 3 servings
Total calories: 1,200
Calories per serving: 400   With Maple Syrup (2 Tbsp/40 g): 500

Carbohydrates:	54 grams	80
Proteins:	19	19
Fat:	12	12

Chapter 12

Marathon Week: Nutrition Preparations

Seven days and counting down to the marathon ... I'll bet you are getting a bit anxious. The good news is, you need not worry about running out of energy and hitting the wall *if* you have done a good job of practicing your fueling before, during and after your long runs. Although 26.2 miles is, indeed, a very long distance to walk or run, optimal fueling will make a *big* difference in your ability to not only finish the marathon but also enjoy it.

For some marathoners, the enjoyment starts with carbohydrate-loading at the pre-marathon pasta party. Yet, carbo-loading means more than just stuffing yourself with pasta. Here's some food for thought.

> **During one of our training meetings, we prepare an 'energy food buffet.' The other coach and I bring a variety of energy bars, gels, and sports drinks. We cut, squirt, and pour so that our marathoners can taste a variety of flavors and textures. By having our buffet, people can sample a wide variety of products. They can then purchase what they think might work for them and try those on their training runs. We constantly remind them: Don't use it in the race if you haven't trained with it!**
>
> *Chris Davis, Joints in Motion coach, Duluth, MN*

Pre-marathon Training Diet

You can't simply eat a big dinner of pasta the night before the marathon and expect to run well. Your muscles have to be receptive to storing the carbohydrates, and that naturally happens as a response to your months of training.

To support the rigors of marathon training, you should have been eating a carbohydrate-rich sports diet *every* day as the foundation for *every* meal. Runners and walkers who have a carbohydrate-based diet (i.e., 55 to 65 percent of the calories from carbohydrates) can train better because their muscles are better fueled. Plus, they can develop a tried-and-true training diet that will support 26.2 miles of marathoning.

The last thing you want to do is change your diet before the marathon. To avoid nutritional mistakes on marathon day, *during training* you should:

- Practice eating your planned pre-marathon breakfast. If you will be traveling a long distance to the marathon, be sure this tried-and-true food will be available on marathon day.
- Start some of your long training runs and walks at the time you'll be running or walking on marathon day. For example, the Boston Marathon starts at noon, so do some training runs at noon. The Disney Marathon in Orlando starts at 6:00 a.m., so do some early morning runs.
- Learn how much pre-exercise food you can eat and then still run or walk comfortably.
- Practice drinking the sports drink that will be available on race day, as well as any mid-run foods (gels, fruit) you plan to eat. (Visit the marathon's website to learn what products will be available and at which mile mark you can expect them.)

These nutrition preparations will help reduce surprises!

The Week Before the Marathon

The biggest change in your schedule during the week before your marathon should be in your *training*, not in your food. You'll want to taper off your training so that your muscles have the opportunity to become fully fueled. Don't bother with any last-minute hard training that will burn off carbohydrates rather than allow them to be stored. Instead, for a Sunday marathon, limit yourself to four miles on Monday and Tuesday, rest on Wednesday, three on Thursday, rest on Friday (travel day) and Saturday (light sightseeing).

You need not eat hundreds more calories this week. You simply need to exercise less. This way, the 600 to 1,000 calories you generally expend during training can be used to fuel your muscles. All during this week, you should maintain your tried-and-true high-carbohydrate training diet. Drastic changes commonly lead to upset stomachs, diarrhea, or constipation. For example, carbo-loading on an unusually high amount of fruits and juices might cause diarrhea. Too many white-flour, low-fiber bagels, breads, and pasta might clog your system.

Be sure that you are carbo-loading, not *fat*-loading. Some runners eat two pats of butter per dinner roll, big dollops of sour cream on a potato, and enough dressing to drown a salad. These fatty foods fill the stomach and the fat cells but leave the muscles less fueled. Your best bet is to trade the extra fats for extra carbohydrates:

- Instead of having one roll with butter for 200 calories, have two plain rolls for 200 calories.
- Have pasta with tomato sauce or low-fat sauces rather than oil-based or cheese-based toppings.
- Enjoy low-fat frozen yogurt instead of gourmet ice cream.

Many marathoners totally avoid protein-rich foods the days before the marathon. This is unnecessary because your body still needs protein on a daily basis. Endurance runners even burn a little protein for energy. Hence, you can and should eat a small serving of low-fat proteins, such as poached eggs, yogurt, turkey, or chicken, as the *accompaniment* to the meal (not the main focus), or plant proteins, such as beans and lentils (as your intestines can tolerate them).

The Day Before the Marathon

By now, you may have gained about three to four pounds, but don't panic. This weight gain reflects water weight. For every ounce of carbohydrates stored in your body, you store about three ounces of water. You can tell if your muscles are well saturated with carbohydrates if the scale has gone up two or three pounds.

Instead of relying upon a huge pasta dinner the night before the marathon, you might want to enjoy a substantial carbo-feast at breakfast or lunch. This

There's more to preparing for the marathon than just eating carbs. The marathon is a mind game. You have to program your mind in order to do it.

Hal Gabriel,
Newton MA

Tools for Carbo-loading

When carb-loading, you want to consume about 3 to 5 grams carbohydrates per pound of body weight (6 to 10 g/kg). This amounts to a diet with about 60% of calories from carbohydrates.

Divide your target grams of carbohydrates into three parts of the day:

breakfast + snack   (7:00 a.m. to noon)
lunch + snack   (noon to 5:00 p.m.)
dinner + snack   (5:00 to 10:00 p.m.)

Choose foods to hit your target! You can find carbohydrate info on food labels and websites, such as "www.fitday.com" or "www.calorieking.com".

If you weigh:	Total #g carb/day	Target #g carbs per five hours: 7:00 a.m.-noon; noon-5:00 p.m.; 5:00-10:00 p.m.
100 lbs (45 kg)	300 to 500 g	100 to 175 g
125 lbs (57 kg)	375 to 625 g	125 to 210 g
150 lbs (68 kg)	450 to 750 g	150 to 250 g
175 lbs (80 kg)	525 to 875 g	175 to 290 g

Sample 50 gram carbohydrate choices for the foundation of a meal or snack
- Wheaties, 2 cups (60 g)
- Nature Valley Granola Bar, 2 packets (4 bars; 3 oz; 84 g)
- Thomas' Bagel, 1 (3.5 oz; 100 g)
- Banana, 2 medium (8 oz; 225 g)
- Orange juice, 16 ounces (480 ml)
- Apple, 2 medium (10 oz; 280 g)
- Raisins, 1/2 cup (70 g)
- Pepperidge Farm multi-grain bread, 2.5 slices (75 g)
- Baked potato, 1 large (6.5 ounces; 180 g)
- Pasta, 1 cup cooked (140 g)
- Rice, 1 cup cooked (160 g)
- Fig Newtons, 5 (2.5 oz; 75 g)
- Flavored yogurt (1 cup; 230 g) + 3 graham cracker squares

earlier meal allows plenty of time for the food to move through your system. Or, eat at both times!

You'll be better off eating a little bit too much than too little on the eve of the marathon. But you don't want to overeat either. Learning the right balance takes practice. Let each preparatory race and long run be opportunities to learn.

Be sure to drink extra water, juices, and even carbohydrate-rich soft drinks, if desired. Abstain from too much wine, beer, and other alcoholic beverages. While one glass of wine or a can of beer may be OK, particularly if you consume it along with a carb-based meal and water, two or three drinks can hurt your ability to perform well the next day. Your best bet is to be well saturated with water, not hungover with alcohol.

I never eat a very big meal the night before a marathon, as it usually gives me trouble the next day. I prefer to eat a bigger lunch, then a lighter supper.

Grete Waitz, Norway

Marathon Morning

With luck, you'll wake up to a clear, crisp day that makes you want to jump out of bed and walk or run! Before embarking upon your day's task, be sure to eat breakfast. One of the biggest nutritional mistakes made by novice marathoners is eating too little beforehand, fearing that eating will result in an upset stomach.

As I've repeatedly mentioned, be sure to eat pre-marathon foods that are tried-and-true. That is, don't feast on a pancake breakfast marathon morning only to discover that pancakes settle like lead bricks. Some marathoners can eat a bagel, juice, or about 500 calories of a breakfast one to three hours before the event; many carry familiar foods with them to the pre-race "athletes' village." Others want more time for their stomach to empty; they've learned they run best if they wake up at 4 a.m., eat a bowl of oatmeal, then go back to bed.

Here are some examples of simple 500-calorie pre-marathon breakfasts. You might want more (or fewer) calories, depending on your body size and tolerance to food:

Oatmeal, 2 packets made with	300 calories
Milk, 1 cup low-fat (240 ml)	100
Banana, medium	100

Bagel (Dunkin Donuts)	300
Peanut butter, 2 Tbsp (30 g)	200

PowerBar, 1	230
Yogurt, flavored	250
Gatorade, 8 oz (240 ml)	50

Eggs, 2 poached on	150
Toast, 2 slices	200
Orange juice, 12 oz (360 ml)	150

Two Sample Carbo-loading Food Plans (3,200-3,400 Calories)

These menus are appropriate for a 150 pound (68 kg) athlete who needs about 4 grams of carbs per pound of body weight (8 g/kg) to adequately carbo-load.

	Approximate Calories	Carbs (g)
Wheaties, 2 cups (60 g)	220	48
Milk, 1% lowfat, 8 oz (240 ml)	100	12
Bagel, 1 (3.5 oz; 100 g)	300	55
Honey, 1 Tbsp (20 g)	60	17
Orange juice, 12 oz (360 ml)	160	40
Breakfast: 830 cals, 75% carb		
Whole grain bread, 2 slices (60 g)	200	40
Peanut butter, 2 Tbsp (30 g)	200	8
Jelly, 2 Tbsp (30 g)	100	25
Fruit yogurt, 8 oz (240 ml)	230	35
Pretzels, 2 oz (60 g)	230	48
Lunch: 970 cals, 65% carb		
Apple, 1 large (7 oz; 120 g)	120	30
Graham crackers, 4 squares	120	22
Snack total: 240 cals; 90% carb		
Chicken breast, 5 oz (140 g)	250	–
Rice, 1.5 cups cooked (240 g)	300	65
Broccoli, 1 cup (180 g)	50	10
Dinner rolls, 2 whole wheat (2 oz; 60 g)	200	40
Dinner: 800 cals; 60% carb		
Banana, 1 medium (4 oz; 120 g))	100	25
Sherbert, 1 cup; (240 ml)	260	45
p.m. snack: 360 cals, ~ 100% carb		
TOTAL Menu #1	**3,200**	**563 g**
~ 70% carb; ~ 4 g carb/lb for a 150 lb athlete		

Menu #2

Oatmeal, 1 cup dry (3 oz; 85 g), cooked in	300	55
Milk. 16 ounces (480 ml)	200	25
Raisins, 1/4 cup (35 g)	130	30
Brown sugar, 1.5 Tbsp (15 g)	50	12
Apple juice, 8 oz. (240 ml)	120	30

Breakfast: 800 cals; 75% carb

Sub sandwich roll, 6" (4 oz; 110 g)	320	60
Lean meat (4 oz; 110 g)	200	–
Fruit yogurt, 8 oz (240 ml)	240	40
Grape juice, 12 oz (360 ml)	220	55

Lunch: 980 cals; 80% carb

Fig Newtons, 6	330	65
Jelly beans, 15 large (1.5 oz; 45 g)	150	38

Snack: 480 cals; 85% carb

Spaghetti. 2 cups cooked (280 g)	400	80
Prego spaghetti sauce, 1 cup (250 g)	250	40
Italian bread, 2 slices(1.5 oz; 45 g)	150	30
Root beer, 12 ounces (360 ml)	140	38

Dinner: 940 cals; 80% carb

Canned peaches in syrup, 1 cup (260 g) 200
48   Snack: 200 cals; ~100% carb

TOTAL Menu #2	**3,400**	**646 g**

~ 75% carb; ~ 4.5 g carb/lb for a 150 lb athlete

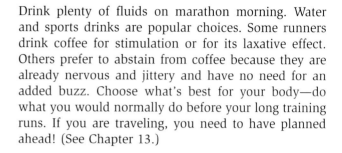

> I drink coffee before a marathon, just like I drink coffee every day. It's a part of my normal routine. I like coffee not because it boosts my energy but rather because it helps me go to the bathroom.

Bill Rodgers, Boston, MA

Drink plenty of fluids on marathon morning. Water and sports drinks are popular choices. Some runners drink coffee for stimulation or for its laxative effect. Others prefer to abstain from coffee because they are already nervous and jittery and have no need for an added buzz. Choose what's best for your body—do what you would normally do before your long training runs. If you are traveling, you need to have planned ahead! (See Chapter 13.)

Whatever beverage you like to drink, take it with you in a throw-away bottle so you'll have it available at the race. Because water takes about 45 to 90 minutes to move through your system, you can drink several glasses up to two hours before the marathon, have time to urinate the excess, then tank up again 5 to 15 minutes before the starting gun. With pre-race nerves, don't be surprised if you are urinating twenty times!

Fueling During the Marathon

Your job during the marathon is to prevent dehydration and to maintain a normal blood sugar level. I have discussed those topics in Chapters 8, 9, and 10. Remember, you should be doing nothing new, special, or different during the marathon. Stick with what has worked for you in your training runs. That is, stick with the tried-and-true.

Summary

By marathon day, you should be well trained. You should have not only strong muscles but also a strong knowledge of the foods and fluids you need to fuel those muscles. Knowing you are nutritionally prepared, you need not fear that you will tire prematurely, or "hit the wall." Instead, you can focus on the day's job – to enjoy the 26.2 miles with energy to spare!

Easy Lasagna

This recipe is "easy" because it eliminates the step of cooking the lasagna noodles before assembly.

When eating this lasagna pre-event, be aware that almost half the calories come from protein and fat. (Most lasagnas are even higher in protein and fat!) Be sure to round out the meal with (whole grain) rolls, fruit salad, juice and other carbohydrate-rich foods.

1 pound (2 cups; 500 g) part-skim ricotta or cottage cheese or a mixture
1 egg or substitute
1 teaspoon (1.5 g) dried oregano
1 teaspoon (5 g) salt, as desired
1 48-ounce (1,345 g) jar spaghetti sauce
2 cups (480 ml) water
20 lasagna noodles (a one-pound (450 g) box has 24 noodles)
4 to 6 ounces (1 to 1 1/2 cups; 120 to 180 g) mozarella cheese, shredded

Optional: Your choice of –
1 10-ounce (300 g) package frozen chopped spinach, thawed and drained
4 cups (1 liter) diced vegetables (onions, mushrooms. carrots, zucchini, summer squash, etc.) steamed or sauted in a little oil
1 pound (450 g) extra-lean hamburger or ground turkey, browned and drained
1 pound (450 g) tofu, crumbled

1. In a bowl, mix the ricotta cheese with the egg, spinach, oregano, salt (and vegetables and meat).
2. In a 9" x 13" lasagna pan (23 x 38 cm), place some sauce, then a layer of 4 uncooked lasagna noodles. Add a layer of cheese/vegetable mixture, then spaghetti sauce. Repeat three times, ending with noodles. Sprinkle shredded mozarella over the top.
3. Pour the 2 cups of water around the edges. Cover tightly with foil and bake at 350°F (175°C) for about 1 hour and 15 minutes, uncovering for the last 10 minutes. (Try to prevent the foil from sticking to the top cheese by covering it carefully.

Yield: 8 servings
Total calories: 3,700
Calories per serving: 460

Carbohydrates 64 grams
Protein 22 grams
Fat 13 grams

Carb-loading Menu

	calories	carbs
1 serving lasagna	460 calories	64 g carbs
French bread (2 oz; 60 g)	150	25
Fruit salad, bowl	140	35
Cranapple juice, 8 oz (240 g)	150	38
Total:	**900 calories**	

162 g carbs (72% calories from carbohydrates)

Chapter 13

Tips for the Traveling Marathoner

When I traveled to marathons, I'd eat the pasta dinner, then go back to the hotel room, where I'd relax on the bed, watch TV, and carbo-load on a stack of Fig Newtons and a quart of orange juice. Not everyone can handle that many Fig Newtons, but they sure worked for me and helped give me my best times!

Gerry Beagan, Cranston, RI

Participating in a marathon that is far away from your home provides a fun excuse to travel. But once you arrive at the host location, be sure to fight the urge to do too much pre-marathon sightseeing. All too often when traveling, you can get side-tracked by the confusion and excitement of being in a new city. Better yet, save the sightseeing until *after* the event.

Your first priority is to put your feet up, rest your legs, relax with some juice and some other tried-and-true carbohydrates, and visualize yourself completing the entire marathon smoothly, strongly, and successfully. You'll also want to figure out how you are going to best fuel yourself. Some marathoners travel with a cooler packed with abundant tried-and-true meals and snacks. Others confront the nutritional challenges of finding familiar sports foods at local restaurants—and avoiding the rich temptations that lurk in every bakery, deli, and dessert cart. To help you better accommodate a high-carbohydrate sports diet into your traveling routine, here are a few tips.

Breakfast:

- At a restaurant, order pancakes, French toast, whole-wheat toast, or English, bran, or corn muffins. Add jelly, jam, or maple syrup for extra carbohydrates, but hold the butter or request that it be served on the side so that you can better control the amount of fat in your meal.
- Order a *large* orange juice or tomato juice. This can help compensate for a potential lack of fruits or veggies in the other meals. For a hotel stay, you might want to save time and money by packing your own cereal, raisins, and spoon. Either bring powdered milk or buy a half-pint of low-fat milk at a local convenience store. A water glass or milk carton can double as a cereal bowl.

Plan on bringing what you need to the marathon. Do not assume the event will supply you with what you are accustomed to eating. You have spent six months preparing for this marathon; do not jeopardize your ability to enjoy it by eating some unfamiliar food.

Matt Keil, Team in Training coach, San Jose, CA

Lunch:

- Find a deli or restaurant that offers wholesome breads. Request a sandwich that emphasizes the bread, rather than the filling (preferably lean beef, turkey, ham, or chicken). Hold the mayonnaise, and instead, add moistness with mustard or ketchup, sliced tomatoes, and lettuce. Add more carbohydrates with juice, fruit, fig bars (brought from a corner store), or yogurt for dessert.
- At fast-food restaurants, the burgers, fried fish, special sandwiches, and French fries have a very high fat content. You'll get more carbohydrates by sticking to the spaghetti, baked potatoes, chili, or thick-crust pizza selections.

Packing Your Cooler

One key to successfully selecting a top-notch sports diet when you are traveling is to bring some foods with you. For example, you might want to bring items for before, during and after the marathon:

Pre-marathon:
Bagels
Bananas
Peanut butter
Energy bars
Instant oatmeal
Raisins
Coffee or tea bags

During the marathon:
Gels
Clif Bloks
Sports beans
Hard candy
Twizzlers
Peppermint patties
Dried fruit

Post marathon:
Ginger ale or cola (in case you feel sick)
V-8 juice (for salt)
Fruit yogurt or Go-gurt (protein-carb combo)
Cup of soup (fluid, salt, carbs)
Salted nuts (protein, salt)
Chocolate chip cookies (treat!)

Some runners choose a hotel with a microwave oven in the bedroom; others travel with an electric tea kettle for hot water (coffee, instant oatmeal, cup-of-soup). This is not foolproof, however. For example, elite marathoner Gelindo Bordin of Italy (known as a food-lover extraordinaire) schlepped not only his own pasta and grateable hard cheese to New York for the marathon, but also a small hot plate on which to cook in his hotel. The only problem was that the water was different in New York City. To his dismay, this not only affected his cooking but also negated his beloved espresso.

The 1992 New York City Marathon winner, Willie Mtolo of South Africa, also brought a hot plate to cook his traditional pre-marathon food: phutu, a cornmeal-based porridge. His cooking, however, promptly set off the hotel's fire detectors. Mtolo and his fiancée used towels to fan the smoke out the windows, waited for the firefighters to leave, then finished their meal in peace. Such can be the price of eating your familiar foods in preparation for the marathon!

- Request thick-crust pizza (with veggie toppings) rather than thin-crust pizza with pepperoni or sausage.
- At a salad bar, generously pile on the chickpeas, three-bean salad, beets, and fat-free croutons. Take plenty of bread. But don't fat-load on large amounts of butter, salad dressings, or mayonnaise-smothered pasta and potato salads.
- Baked potatoes are a super choice if you request them plain rather than drenched with butter, sour cream, and cheese toppings. For moistness, try mashing the potato with milk (special request) rather than butter, or eat them with ketchup.
- Hearty soups (such as split pea, minestrone, lentil, vegetable, or noodle) accompanied by crackers, bread, a plain bagel, or an English muffin provide a satisfying, carbohydrate-rich, low-fat meal.
- Both juices and soft drinks are rich in carbohydrates. Juices, however, are nutritionally preferable for vitamin C, potassium, and wholesome goodness.

Dinner:
- If possible, check out the restaurant beforehand to make sure that it offers wholesome carbohydrates (pasta, baked potatoes, rice, steamed vegetables, salad bars, homemade breads, fruit, juice), broiled foods, and low-fat options. To be on the safe side, save the exotic restaurants for *after* the marathon! Inquire how dishes are made. Request they be prepared with minimal fat.
- Eat the breads and rolls either plain or with jelly. Replace the butter calories with high-carbohydrate choices: another slice of bread, a second potato, soup and crackers, juice, sherbet, or frozen yogurt.
- When ordering salads, always request the dressing be served on the side. Otherwise, you may get as many as 400 calories of oil or mayonnaise—fatty foods that fill your stomach but leave your muscles unfueled.

Temptations for Travelers

Traveling marathoners can easily fat-load instead of carbo-load. Wisely choose your pre-marthon snacks and meals!

Temptation	Calories	% calories from fat	grams fat
Cinnabon	670	47%	34
Big Mac	560	48%	30
Pizza Hut Personal Pan Pizza,			30
Pepperoni	660	41%	
Au Bon Pain Chicken			
Caesar Wrap	590	37%	22
Mrs. Field's Oatmeal			
Chocolate Chip Cookie	280	42%	13
Cheesecake Factory,			
1 slice, original	710	62%	49

Snacks and Munchies:
- Pack your own snacks. Some suggestions include: whole-grain bagels, muffins, rolls, crackers, pretzels, fig bars, energy bars, granola bars, oatmeal-raisin cookies, graham crackers, oranges, raisins, dried or fresh fruit, and juice boxes.
- Buy wholesome snacks at a convenience store: small packets of trail mix, bananas, dried fruit, yogurt, V-8 juice or fruit juice, bagel, hot pretzel, slice of thick-crust pizza, small sandwich, or cup of soup.

Summary

Traveling is fun but filled with food temptations. Do your best to stick to tried-and-true foods that you know will settle well and not upset your digestive system. Save the food experimentation until *after* the marathon. If you have any doubts about the availability of familiar foods, plan ahead and bring some "safe" foods with you—including the gels, energy bars, and sports foods you will want to consume during the marathon itself.

Breakfast for Travelers

If you're heading for a race out of town, this breakfast is portable, easy, and substantial. You can mix and match your own combinations of fruits and cereals.

In a plastic container with a lid, combine:
1/4 cup (40 g) raw rolled oats
1/4 cup (30 g) Grape-Nuts cereal or other cereal
1/4 cup (35 g) raisins or other dried fruit
1/2 cup (35 g) dry non-fat milk powder

When you are ready to eat, simply add 1 cup (240 ml) of cold water and shake!

YIELD: 1 serving
Calories per serving: 700

	Grams
Carbohydrates:	135
Protein:	35
Fat:	3

Chapter 14

Calculating Your Calorie Needs

Many marathoners are on the "see-food diet"; they see food and they eat it. They can naturally regulate a proper calorie intake and have little need to calculate calories. They simply eat when they are hungry and stop when they are content. But other marathoners see food and try to not eat it. They deem food as "fattening" and counter to their desires to be leaner, lighter runners. They have lost touch with their body's natural ability to regulate an appropriate food intake. They often do not eat when they are hungry (such happens with severe reducing diets or skipping meals) and then overeat later in the day.

As a marathoner, you should eat your calories evenly throughout the day, not in a crescendo. That is, don't skimp on daytime meals only to spend your whole calorie budget in the evening! The better bet is to budget your calories so you eat *enough* at breakfast and lunch to support both an active life and a rigorous training program. Eating (wholesome) calories evenly throughout the day invests in high energy, added stamina, strength, and smooth running, to say nothing of better health.

If you struggle with energy lags, you might wonder how much food—that is, how many calories—are OK to eat to boost energy yet not "get fat." Just as you have a monetary budget that limits how much money you can spend when you go shopping, knowing your calorie budget can help you estimate how many calories are appropriate to:

- lose desired weight and maintain energy for running
- eat at each meal so you can avoid energy lags
- fuel-up and refuel from workouts
- feel energetic, train better, and feel good about your eating.

Once educated, most marathoners can naturally regulate their food intake—without counting calories.

A calorie-counting approach to eating can be particularly helpful to marathoners who feel tired all the time. It can help you understand why you are tired. For example, if you skip breakfast and lunch (i.e., eat zero calories, zero fuel), you can clearly see why you lack energy for your afternoon training session. If you are weight-conscious, calorie information allows you to determine how much food you can eat for fuel yet still lose body fat.

Calculating Your Calorie Needs

Here's an easy formula to help you estimate your calorie needs. For more personalized advice, I highly recommend you consult with a registered dietitian who specializes in sports nutrition. Visit the American Dietetic Association's referral network at www.eatright.org to find a local sports dietitian.

1. To estimate your resting metabolic rate (RMR), that is, the amount of calories you need to simply breathe, pump blood, and be alive:

Multiply your weight (or a good weight for your body) by 10 calories per pound (or 22 calories per kilogram).
_____weight (lbs) x 10 calories/lb = _____ calories for your RMR

1450

Example: If you weigh 120 pounds, you need approximately 1,200 calories (120 x 10) to simply do nothing all day except exist. If you are significantly overweight, use an adjusted weight: the weight that is half-way between your desired weight and your current weight.

2. Add more calories for daily activity—apart from your running and other purposeful exercise.
- 50% x RMR if you are moderately active throughout the day
- ~30-40% if you are sedentary
- ~60-70% if you are very active (apart from your running or walking)

50% x _____RMR = _____ calories for moderate daily activity

Example: A moderately active 120-pound woman who requires 1,200 calories for her resting metabolic rate needs about 600 more calories for activities of daily living. This totals 1,800 calories per day—without running.

3. Add more calories for your purposeful exercise. The general rule of thumb is 100 calories per mile, but more precisely, this depends upon your weight.

Body Weight	Calories per mile (1,6 km)
lbs (kg)	
120 (55)	95
140 (64)	110
160 (73)	125
180 (82)	140

____exercise calories + _____daily activity + _____RMR = _____total calories

Example: A 120-pound woman who runs five miles per day burns about 475 calories while running. This brings her to about 2,275 calories per day to maintain her weight (475 running + 600 moderate daily activity + 1,200 RMR = 2.275). For simplicity, let's just say 2,300 calories.

Note: After a very hard workout or long run, marathoners tend to rest, recover and burn fewer calories than usual during the rest of their day. Observe if this happens with you. That is, if you tend to sit more than usual—reading more or watching more TV—after having done a long weekend run, adjust your calorie needs accordingly!

4. To lose weight, target 80 percent of total calorie needs.
80% x _____total calories = _____ calories to reduce weight

Example: .80 x 2,300 calories = 1,840 calories, or more simply 1,800 calories/day

(Refer to Chapter 15 for more guidance on weight loss.)

5. Now, take your calorie budget and divide it into three or four parts of the day. For the 120-pound woman on a diet, this comes to:

	Calories			Calories
Breakfast/snack	600	OR	Breakfast	500
Lunch/snack	600		Lunch	500
Dinner/snack	600		Lunch #2	300
			Dinner	500

The next step is to read food labels and get calorie information from websites (www.fitday.com, www.calorieking.com) to become familiar with the calorie content of the foods you commonly eat and then fuel your body according to the rules for a well-balanced diet.

Honor Hunger

I commonly hear marathoners complain "Ever since I started training longer distances, I've been hungry all the time." They often feel confused by hunger and sometimes even feel guilty they are always eager to eat. One walker perceived her hunger as being bad and wrong.

Hunger is normal; it is simply your body's way of talking to you, requesting fuel. After all, the more you exercise, the hungrier you will get and the more fuel you need. Plan to fuel up or refuel at least every four hours. You should not spend your day feeling hungry—even if you are on a reducing diet (see Chapter 15). If your 8:00 a.m. breakfast finds you hungry earlier than noon, your breakfast simply contained too few calories. You need a supplemental midmorning snack or a bigger breakfast that supplies about one-third of your day's calories.

Come noontime, instead of thinking something is wrong with you because you are hungry again, enjoy lunch as being the second-most-important meal of

Calorie Needs of Marathoners

Here are approximate calorie needs for marathoners of different weights who remain moderately active throughout the day. Take note: After a 10-miler, you may be ready to nap the rest of the day, and that would reduce your calorie needs! Be sure to adjust your calories according to your 24-hour energy expenditure.

Weight lbs (kg)	Approximate calorie needs for: daily living	5 mile-run or walk	10-mile run or walk
120 (55)	1,800	2,300	2,700
140 (64)	2,100	2,650	3,200
160 (73)	2,400	3,000	3,650
180 (82)	2,700	3,400	4,100

the day. Morning runners, in particular, need a hearty lunch to refuel their muscles; afternoon runners need a respectable lunch and afternoon snack/second lunch to fuel for their after-work training.

Whereas some runners like to satisfy their appetites with big meals, others prefer to divide their calories into mini-meals eaten every two hours. Eat however suits your training schedule and lifestyle. But whatever you do, eat when you are physically hungry. Hunger is simply your body's request for fuel. (The next chapter offers strategies for managing food that is mis-used as a "drug" to calm and reward yourself; keep reading!)

Banana Frostie

Whenever you are confronted with a surplus of bananas that are getting too ripe, peel them, cut them into chunks, and freeze them. Then, they'll be ready and waiting to be whipped into this frosty treat that tastes sinfully good. You'll think you are eating ice cream, but you are actually sneaking extra milk and fruit into your food plan!

Enjoy this as a yummy protein-carb recovery beverage.

Banana, in frozen chunks
1 cup (240 ml) lowfat milk

Optional: honey, brown sugar, or sugar substitute; dash of cinnamon, 1/4 teaspoon (1 ml) vanilla extract.

* Put the frozen banana chunks into a blender with milk.
* Blend on medium speed until smooth.
* Add sweetener and flavorings, as desired

Yield: 1 serving
Total calories: 230

Carbohydrates: 40 grams
Protein: 8 grams
Fat: 4 grams

Chapter 15

Weight Reduction for Marathoners

Many overweight people commit to walking or running a marathon with hopes of killing two birds with one stone:

1. getting fit and healthy
2. losing undesired body fat.

Much to their dismay, they get fit, but some remain fatter than desired. As coach Lloyd Burnett of Mission, TX, said, "I once trained three new marathoners who each lost 20 pounds in less than 6 months. Each of them made the commitment to be conscious about their calories and overall food intake. My training partner and I, on the other hand, have run almost 20 marathons but we each still weigh 220 pounds. I love my beer and he loves his tortillas. We're not willing to commit to the diet part of the event, even though we see the results all around us.

> I have been walking marathons for two years. Like the majority of walkers, I was hoping to lose weight, but that has not been the case for me. Many of my walking friends have even gained weight. Exercise alone does not suffice!
>
> *Becky Goodrum,*
> *Cleveland, OH*

How to Lose Weight and Have Energy to Exercise

I spend hours helping marathoners who struggle to lose weight. Most feel frustrated they just can't seem to shed those final few pounds. Inevitably, the first words they say to me are, "I know what I *should* do to lose weight. I just can't do it." They think they should follow a strict diet with rigid rules and regulations.

Wrong. Diets don't work. If diets did work, every marathoner would be as thin as desired. The key to losing weight is to:

• stop thinking about *going on a diet*
• start learning *how to eat healthfully*

If you are dieting by day, only to overeat at night, think again.

> I suggest that people spend a year trying all the different diets they can find. Then, after having no success at achieving their goals, they gradually modify their normal eating habits. There are no quick fixes for weight loss. Period. Show me a quick fix, and I will show you how you are hurting your body.
>
> *John Correia,*
> *San Diego, CA*

How Much Is OK to Eat?

As was outlined in Chapter 14, active people need more than just a few calories to fuel themselves. To determine just how much you can appropriately eat, refer back to page 122. Note that your body requires an amazing amount of energy to pump blood, breathe, produce urine, grow hair, and simply exist. (Also note that you deserve to eat those maintenance calories even if you are injured and unable to run.)

Weight Expectations

Although only nature knows the best weight for your body, the following guidelines offer a very general method to estimate a healthy weight. For a weight range, add or subtract 10 percent, according to your body frame and musculature. (These guidelines do not work for very muscular athletes.)

Women: 100 pounds (45 kg) for the first 5 feet (1.52 m) of height;
5 pounds (2.3 kg) per inch (2.5 cm) thereafter

Example: A woman who is 5'6" could appropriately weigh 130 lbs, or 117 lbs at the lower end if she is petite, or 143 lbs if she is muscular. (1.7 m; 59 kg, 53-65 kg)

Men: 106 pounds (48 kg) for the first 5 feet (1.52 m) of height;
6 pounds (2.7 kg) per inch (2.5 cm) thereafter

Example: A man who is 5'10" could appropriately weigh 166 lbs, or 150 lbs at the lower end if he is petite, or 182 lbs if he is muscular. (1.8 m; 75.5 kg, 68-83 kg)

Although marathoners commonly want to be lighter than the average person, heed this message: If you are striving to weigh significantly less than the weight estimated by this general guideline, think again. Pay attention to the genetic design for your body and don't struggle to get too light. The best weight goal is to be fit and healthy rather than sleek and skinny. Even heavy marathoners can be fit and healthy!

An appropriate reducing diet knocks off only *20 percent or less of your calorie needs.* Many weight-conscious marathoners try to eat as little as possible. That's a big mistake. Perhaps the following case study will help you understand why.

Ann, a 120-pound (54.5 kg) nurse, walks 5 miles most days. She requires about 2,200 to 2,300 calories to maintain her weight:

- 1,200 calories for her resting metabolic rate (10 calories per pound x 120 pounds)
- 600 calories for general daily activity (50% x 1,200 calories)
- 475 calories for her walk (95 calories per mile x 5 miles)

To appropriately lose weight, I recommended she cut her total calorie intake by 20 percent (about 400 to 500 calories), leaving her with 1,800 calories for her reducing plan.

To Ann, 1,800 sounded like too many calories. She exclaimed "I could never eat that much without turning into a blimp. If I can't lose weight when I'm on a 1,000-calorie diet, how could I possibly do so on 1,800? My metabolism is *so slow*. I seem to gain weight just smelling cookies."

Although Ann challenged my calorie recommendations, I suggested that she keep an open mind. The research on athletes' calorie needs suggests very few athletes actually do have slow metabolisms. Researchers have even studied active

> **I frequently see people gain weight during marathon training. They believe the training gives them license to eat anything and everything. Unfortunately, a 300-calorie dessert still shows up on the butt.**
>
> *John Correia,*
> *San Diego CA*

people like Ann who claim to maintain weight despite eating next to nothing. When carefully monitored, these women require the calories one would expect based on standard calculations. Their metabolisms were fine, but they had problems acknowledging how much food they actually ate (or how inactive they were in the non-training part of their day). Their nibbles on grapes, apples, rice cakes, and broken cookies added up! (For more information, refer to *Slow Metabolism Woes* in Chapter 16.)

Because Ann claimed she ate far less than her peers, I suggested she heighten her awareness of her food intake by keeping food records. Food records can be extremely useful to help you understand your eating habits. For example, by listing *everything* that you eat, you might notice that you:

- eat when reading and don't even notice the portion
- eat too little at breakfast and lunch, only to overindulge at night
- diet Monday through Thursday, then splurge on weekends

Accurate food records can help you lose weight because people who keep food records tend to eat about 20 percent less—and that is an appropriate reducing diet!

Five Keys to Successful Weight Reduction

Using your calorie guidelines, you can lose weight with the following five keys to successful weight reduction.

Key #1. Eat just a little bit less. Don't get too hungry or you'll blow your diet. For example, Lori, a receptionist and a runner, tried to self-impose the following bare-bones diet:

Breakfast:	coffee	0 calories
Lunch:	dry salad	100
Snack:	large apple	150
Dinner:	frozen low-calorie meal	300
Total calories:		**550 (until she "blew it")**

This *totaled less than a quarter* of the 2,400 calories she required. No wonder she lacked energy for running. She'd often skip workouts and then at night eat everything in sight, only to get up the next morning with a food hangover. She'd then vow to get back on her diet, skip breakfast, skimp on lunch, lack energy to enjoy running, and blow her diet again at night. Her method was mistaken; her diet was too strict.

If you, like Lori, are trying to lose weight by eating as little as possible and exercising as hard as you can, remember that the less you eat, the more likely you are to blow your diet. Even if you can successfully restrict your intake, the less you eat, the more your body adjusts to having fewer calories. You will start to hibernate similar to what a bear does in winter when food is scarce. That is, your metabolic rate will drop to conserve calories, and you'll feel lethargic, cold, and lack energy to exercise.

Research comparing dieters who either crash-dieted or followed a more reasonable reducing plan showed that both groups lost the same amount of body fat. The strict diet, however, caused the metabolic rate to drop. Why bother to eat next to nothing when you can lose weight with eating just 20 percent less than you need to maintain your weight?

Most of my clients follow 1,800- to 2,200-calorie reduction diets. This is far more than most self-imposed 800- to 1,200-calorie diets. You need a substantial amount of energy to fuel your muscles and have energy to enjoy your training.

For a while I was trying to eat less so that I could weigh less, but I'd end up eating more and weighing more. I finally learned that if I eat sensible meals my weight is fine. I feel better and run better.

Candace Strobach,
Kinnelon, NJ

Key #2. Be sure that you eat more during the day, so that you'll be able to eat less (diet) at night. For an appropriate reducing program, I recommend that you divide your calories evenly throughout the day. Because athletes tend to get hungry at least every four hours, an appropriate reduction diet for a 120-pound female marathoner might be:

Breakfast:	8 a.m.	500 calories
Lunch:	Noon	500
Lunch #2/Snack:	4 p.m.	400
Run:	6 p.m.	
Dinner:	8 p.m.	400

Your goal is to eat on a schedule to *prevent* yourself from getting too hungry. I call this my "eat more, lose weight" food plan.

Your training program may require creative meal scheduling if you exercise during meal times. For example, if you exercise at 6 p.m.—potentially at the height of your hunger—you might better enjoy your training if you eat part of your dinner beforehand. For example, trade in your 200-calorie dinner potato for a 200-calorie bagel at 5:00 p.m. Similarly, if you exercise at 6:00 a.m., you might enjoy greater energy if you eat part of your breakfast beforehand, such as a slice of toast and a glass of juice, and then eat the rest afterwards to recover from the workout and satisfy your hunger. (As I mentioned in Chapter 8, you need to experiment with pre-exercise food to determine the right amount of calories that boost your energy without making you feel heavy and sluggish.)

Some marathoners believe that exercising "on empty"—for example, running first thing in the morning before breakfast—helps them to burn more fat. While this may be true, keep in mind that *burning* fat does not equate *losing* body fat. To lose body fat, you need to have created a calorie *deficit* for the whole day (not just during workouts). People who exercise on empty lack the fuel they need to sustain long, strong workouts. Hence, they burn fewer calories than someone who is properly fueled before exercise. They also experience extreme hunger later on

Fuel by Day; Diet by Night!

If blown diets are your downfall, I recommend you take the following steps:

Eat a bigger breakfast and lunch—and observe the benefits (more energy, less hunger during the day and after dinner, better workouts).

Enjoy a substantial afternoon snack or second lunch that ruins your evening appetite.

"Diet" at night by eating smaller portions than usual.

and often get derailed by the Cookie Monster.

Key #3. Eat an appropriate amount of fat. If you are currently eating a high-fat diet filled with butter, mayonnaise, salad dressing, french fries, and pepperoni, you should cut back on these and other fatty foods. Excess dietary fat easily turns into excess body fat, if not clogged arteries.

On the other hand, if you are trying to knock all the fat out of your diet—thinking that if you eat fat, you'll instantly get fat—think again and see Chapter 7. Fat can be helpful for dieters because it takes longer to digest and provides a nice feeling of satisfaction that can prevent you from scrounging around the kitchen, looking for something tasty to eat. Runners who try to eat a no-fat diet commonly live with a nagging hunger, to say nothing of feelings of denial and deprivation.

One study reported that dieters who were instructed to eat 1,200 calories of a high-fat diet actually lost more body fat than the group who were instructed to eat 1,200 calories of a very-low-fat diet. Why? Because the high-fat dieters were better able to comply with their regimen. You, too, may enjoy better success with fat loss if you give yourself reasonable calorie and fat budgets to spend on the foods that you truly enjoy eating. (Refer to Chapter 7 for more information on what 25 percent fat diet looks like.) There is a diet portion of any food—including french fries and cookies!

Why Are You Eating?

Food has many roles. It satisfies hunger, fuels muscles, is a pleasurable part of social gatherings and celebrations, rewards us at the end of a stressful day, and has a calming effect. If you tend to eat for reasons other than fuel, HALT and ask yourself, Why do I want to eat? Is it because I am:

    Hungry?
    Angry or Anxious?
    Lonely?
    Tired?

If you are eating inappropriately, remember that no amount of food will solve any problem. Don't start eating if you know you'll have problems stopping.

Key #4. Try to lose weight when life is smooth. You don't have to lose weight every day. Losing weight requires significant mental energy; you always need to remind yourself, "I'd rather be leaner than eat more calories." Some days you may lack that mental energy. For example, Paul, a lawyer and runner who wanted to lose five pounds before the Chicago Marathon, was stressed out by his demanding work load, training schedule, and family problems. Although he wanted to drop a few pounds, he lacked the mental energy he needed to cut calories. At the end of the day, he'd inevitably succumb to ice cream, his reward for having survived the day.

I reminded Paul that he is only human, with a limited amount of mental and physical energy. Rather than punish himself for lacking energy to restrict calories, he needed to accept the fact that he was stressed and in need of comfort. Like it or not, food provided that comfort.

I recommended that Paul let go of his current goal to *lose* fat and focus instead on *maintaining* his weight and fueling his muscles appropriately. Well-fueled muscles would enhance his running more than would poorly fueled muscles. I also reminded Paul he has the rest of his life to lose excess body fat. In this already stressful time in his life, he might be happier removing the additional self-imposed stress of trying to lose weight. He reluctantly agreed with that reality.

Stressful times are often poor times to try to reduce body fat. Rather, focus on exercising regularly to help cope with stress and on eating healthful foods every four hours to keep your appetite under control. Marathoners who are both stressed and hungry can too easily succumb to overeating. But no amount of food will solve any problem. In fact, it only adds to your feeling out of control.

> Do not be obsessed with the numbers on the scale. With time and training, you will learn at what weight you can perform well. Listening to your body is more accurate than any scale.
>
> *Mike Czech,*
> *Edison, NJ*

Key #5. Have realistic weight goals. Weight is more than a matter of willpower; genetics plays a large role. If you are exercising regularly, fueling appropriately during the day, eating lighter at night, and waking up hankering for breakfast but still have not lost weight, perhaps you have an unrealistic goal? Perhaps you have no excess fat to lose and are already lean for your genetic blueprint? Like it or not, weight is more than a matter of willpower. Although you might wish for a sleeker physique, nature might want you to be more substantial.

Marsha, the novice marathoner, was short and had thin hair and big thighs, "just like my mothers and sisters." Although she put no effort into trying to grow taller or thicken her hair, she obsessed about the fat on her thighs and spent lots of energy trying to reduce them.

I reminded Marsha that although she could remodel her body to a certain extent, she couldn't totally redesign it. Plain and simple, walkers and runners, like fruits, come in varying sizes and shapes. No one body type is right or wrong.

In order to determine an appropriate weight for your body, I recommend you stop looking at the scale and start looking at your family. Imagine yourself at a family reunion.

- How do you compare to other members of your family?
- Are you currently leaner than they are? fatter? the same?
- If leaner, are you struggling to stay that way?

If you are significantly leaner, you may already be underweight for your body.

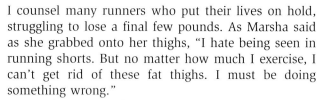

Planned weight loss—one to two pounds per week—and marathon training don't mix. The weight loss should occur prior to or during the early stages of the training program. Once mileage and quality of training increase, the nutrition focus should be on replenishment, not deficit, of calories.

Ronnie Carda,
Madison, WI

I counsel many runners who put their lives on hold, struggling to lose a final few pounds. As Marsha said as she grabbed onto her thighs, "I hate being seen in running shorts. But no matter how much I exercise, I can't get rid of these fat thighs. I must be doing something wrong."

Marsha was simply trying to get to a weight that was abnormal for her genetics. She was already leaner than other members of her family. I helped her to understand the reason why women (as compared to men) have "fat thighs": the fat in the thigh area is sex-specific. It is a storehouse of energy for potential pregnancy and breast feeding and is supposed to be there. Just as women have breast tissue, women also have thigh tissue. Women have fatter thighs than men because women are women. Marsha needed to accept the realities of being a woman and stop comparing herself to the magazine models who indeed have rare physiques.

If you are wasting your time and energy complaining about your body, keep this in perspective: Life is a gift, too short to be spent obsessing about food and weight. Be appreciative of all our body can do for you—such as endure marathon training—and stop criticizing your body for what it is not. You can be fit, healthy and happy at any size. You can also be miserable at your "perfect weight" if the cost of attaining that weight is yo-yo dieting, poor nutrition, lack of energy to exercise, guilt for eating, a sense of failure that crushes your self-esteem: and, of course, poor marathon performance.

Summary

Food is fuel. You need to fuel your muscles appropriately even if you are trying to lose weight. Be realistic about your expectations and remember:
- the thinnest marathoner may not be the fastest marathoner
- the best fueled marathoners will always win with good nutrition

Also remember the following keys to successful weight control:
1. Deduct only 20 percent (or less) of your calorie budget; don't starve yourself.
2. Fuel during the day, then diet at night. Morning hunger can be a sign you lost weight overnight.
3. Include a little bit of (healthful) fat at each meal to keep you from feeling hungry and also from feeling denied.
4. Strive to maintain weight on stress-filled days and lose weight on gentler days.
5. Honor your genetics and be realistic with your weight goals.

Brenda's Greek Salad

Salads are a good food for dieters because you can get lots of chews for few calories—that is, unless the salad is smothered with dressing. This recipe uses a little feta as the "dressing" and is a favorite of Brenda Ponichtera RD, cookbook author of *"Quick and Healthy Recipes and Ideas: For people who say they don't have time to cook healthy meals,"* www.quickandhealthy.net.

If time allows, let the salad marinate for several hours and make enough for leftovers because it'll be great the next day. (I like to make it into a wrap for lunch!) For a richer flavor, you can add a drizzle of olive oil.

Note: The salad can be made with only green peppers; it'll taste just fine.

1 green pepper, sliced
1 red pepper, sliced
1 yellow pepper, sliced
1 unpeeled cucumber, sliced
2 tablespoons (30 g) lemon juice
3 tablespoons (45 g) red wine vinegar
1/4 teaspoon (1 g) dried oregano
4 ounces (120 g) feta cheese, crumbled

1. Mix peppers and cucumber in a bowl.
2. Add lemon juice, vinegar, and oregano. Mix well.
3. Top with crumbled feta cheese.

Yield: 4 servings
Total calories: 400

Calories per serving: 100 calories
Carbohydrates: 8 grams
Protein: 5 grams
Fat: 6 grams

™ Brenda J. Ponichtera, RD Reprinted with permission from *Quick & Healthy Recipes and Ideas* (ScaleDown Publishing, Inc.).

Chapter 16

Dieting Gone Awry

Fueled by the "thinner is better" philosophy, some marathoners consider food to be a fattening enemy rather than a friendly fuel. With the fear that eating satisfying meals will make them fatter and slower, some weight-conscious marathoners deny themselves permission to eat adequately until they lose those final few pounds ... an elusive goal.

Marathoners who strive to be "perfectly" thin commonly pay a high price: poor nutrition, poorly fueled muscles, stress fractures, nagging injuries, loss of menses (in women), to say nothing of reduced stamina, endurance, and performance. In their overconcern about their bodies, dieting marathoners forget this formula:

appropriate eating + regular exercise = appropriate weight

Whereas Chapter 15 offered guidance about how to lose weight and maintain energy for walking or running, this chapter will provide an additional perspective to help resolve the obsessions with food and weight that happen when dieting goes awry. These obsessions are most common in active women. Hence this chapter focuses mostly on women, but if you are a man who struggles with food, the information can help you, as well.

Women and Weight

Why is weight such a big issue among women? Let's look at the possible explanations.

1. Women naturally have more body fat than men, and many women deem this as undesireable. Never-the-less, women need more body fat to:
- protect their ability to create and nourish healthy babies
- provide a storehouse of calories for pregnancy and breast feeding

This essential body fat is stored not only in the breasts but also in the hips, abdomen, and upper legs. That's why women tend to have heavier thighs than most men.

Whereas 11 to 13 percent of a woman's body weight is essential fat stores, only 3 to 5 percent of a man's body weight is essential body fat. Hence, women who try to achieve the "cut look" of male athletes commonly end up having to starve themselves, then they binge and obsess about food as they struggle to attain an unnatural image.

Surveys of top women athletes suggest even the very lean, front-of-the-pack women runners wish they could be lighter. No wonder dieting and disordered eating patterns prevail! The majority of male runners, in comparison, seem to be more at peace with their natural weight and, consequently, are more at peace with food.

2. Women tend to have distorted body images. The Madison Avenue image that adorns every storefront and magazine ad leads us to believe that nature makes all women universally lean. Any aberration is thought to be a result of gluttony and lack of willpower. Wrong!

Nature makes us in different sizes and shapes, like it or not. If all the marathoners who are discontent with their weight could only learn to accept and love their bodies as being "good enough," eating disorders would be rare. Case in point, a food-obsessed 5'7" and 115-pound marathoner lamented, "I don't have the gaunt look of the really fast runners. I really wish I could weigh 110." She was unable to see that she was already very lean; a normal, healthy weight for a 5'7" woman is 135 pounds! She was training harder and harder to burn calories and lose body fat. Her running contrasted with that of other runners, commonly men, who train primarily to enhance performance, not to burn fat and reshape their bodies.

The Slow Metabolism Woes

Some marathoners comment the fitter they are, the fewer calories they need. They perceive themselves as being energy-efficient; they commonly complain about being cold all the time, feeling lethargic, and (among women) lacking regular menstrual cycles. As elite runner Priscilla Welch once said, "I'm amazed at what nonrunners can tuck away." Perhaps you've heard your buddies express similar complaints:

- I eat less than my friends, but I still don't lose weight. There must be something wrong with my metabolism.
- I maintain weight on only 1,000 calories per day. I want to lose a few pounds, but I can't imagine eating any less.
- I run at least eight miles every day and eat only one meal a day. I can't understand why I don't lose weight.

These comments raise questions about metabolic efficiency. Does nature slow an athlete's metabolism to protect him or her from getting too thin?

According to Dr. Jack Wilmore, exercise physiologist at the University of Texas at Austin, the energy-efficient athlete does not exist. His research suggests that metabolic rate is closely tied to muscle mass (Wilmore, 1992). Many of the marathoners who restrict calories end up burning muscle tissue for energy. Hence, they tend to have less muscle mass. Consequently, they require fewer calories. "Plain and simple, athletes who have well-developed muscles require more calories than those who have less muscle."

Often overlooked is how few calories a marathoner burns when he or she is not exercising. After a long run, marathoners can easily take a nap, read the paper, or relax more than before they started marathon training—when they would have mowed the lawn, played actively with their children, and been more active throughout the entire day. Hence, the trick to reversing "energy efficiency" may be to be active throught the entire day, not just when training.

Women, Running, and Amenorrhea

If you are a marathoner who previously had regular menstrual periods but currently has stopped menstruating, you are experiencing amenorrhea. Although you may think the loss of menses is because you are too thin or are exercising too much, thinness and exercise are generally not the causes of amenorrhea. After all, many very thin marathoners do have regular menses. Studies have shown that both regularly menstruating and amenorrheic athletes commonly have the same amount of body fat.

But the question remains unanswered: Why, given a group of women who have a similar training program and the same low percentage of body fat, do some experience menstrual problems and others don't? Marathoners with amenorrhea often stuggle to maintain an unhealthfully low weight. The cost of achieving this leanness is inadequate nutrition and, consequently, loss of menses.

Athletic amenorrhea is commonly a nutritional problem and sometimes a red flag for an eating disorder. If you stop having regular menstrual periods, be sure to consult with both your gynecologist and sports nutritionist for professional guidance.

Health Risks Associated with Amenorrhea

Although you may deem amenorrhea a desirable side effect of exercise because you no longer have to deal with the hassles and possible discomfort of monthly menstrual periods, amenorrhea can lead to undesirable problems that can interfere with your health and ability to perform at your best. These problems include:

- almost a three times higher incidence of stress fractures
- premature osteoporosis (weakening of the bones) that can effect your bone health in the not-too-distant future
- inability to conceive should you want to have a baby.

If the amenorrhea is caused by very restrictive eating, it can be a symptom of pain and unhappiness in your life. Note that the "absence of at least three consecutive menstrual cycles" is part of the American Psychiatric Association's definition for anorexia.

Amenorrheic women who resume menses can restore some of the bone density lost during their months of amenorrhea, particularly if they are younger than seventeen years. But they do not restore all of it. Your goal should be to minimize the damages of amenorrhea by eating appropriately and taking the proper steps to regain your menstrual periods. Remember: Food is fuel, healthful and health-giving, not a fattening enemy.

Resolving Amenorrhea

The possible changes required to resume menses include:

- training 5 to 15 percent less (50 minutes instead of an hour)
- consuming 10 percent more calories each week, until you ingest an appropriate amount given your activity level. For example, if you have been eating 1,000 calories a day, eat 100 more calories per day for a total of 1,100 total calories a day during the first week (or even for 2 to 3 days); eat a total of 1200 calories per day the second week; 1,300 the third week, and so on. (See Chapter 14 for how to determine an appropriate calorie intake.)

How to Build a Better Food Plan

If you maintain weight despite eating minimal calories and are spending way too much time thinking about food, here's a sample food plan to help you start to fuel your body better. Gradually add 100 calories every 7 days (or every day, for that matter) and observe the benefits: you will likely feel stronger, happier, warmer; sleep better; have bettter workouts and think less about food. Because you are adding essential (not excess) calories to get your body out of hibernation, you will be unlikely to "get fat."

Your best bet to help you through this process of relearning how to eat appropriately, is to go to www.eatright.org or www.SCANdpg.org and use the referral networks to find a local sports dietitian who can provide personalized advice.

1,000 calories		How to increase Baseline Menu: + 100 calories/week X 8 weeks	Improved 1,800-calorie Menu	
Special K, 1 cup (30 g)	100	Week #5. Add 100 cals more cereal	Special K, 2 cups	200
		Week #1. Add banana: + 100 cals	Banana	100
Milk, 1/2 cup	50		Milk 1/2 cup	50
Apple, average	100		Apple	100
		Week #6: Add 14 almonds + 100	Almonds, 14	100
Salad	100		Salad	100
Tuna, small can	100	Week #2. Larger can tuna: + 100 cals	Tuna, lg can	200
		Week #3. Add 1 cup yogurt: + 100	Yogurt, 1 cup	100
		Week #7. Add crackers + 100	Crackers	100
Energy bar	250		Energy bar	250
Chicken breast, 4 oz	200		Chicken breat	200
Broccoli, 2 cups	100		Broccoli, 2 cups	100
		Week #4. Add 1/2 cup rice + 100 cals	Rice, 1/2 cup	100
		Week #8. Add 1 cup milk	Milk, 1 cup	100
Total: 1,000 calories				**1,800**

Some amenorrheic runners have resumed menses with just reduced exercise and no weight gain. For example, an injured runner who totally stops training might resume menses within two months. Others resume menstruating after gaining less than five pounds (rather, rebuilding and restoring five pounds of health). And despite what you may think, this small amount of weight gain tends to include muscle-gain and does not result in your "getting fat."

If you have stopped menstruating and believe that poor eating may be part of the problem, you should consider getting a nutrition checkup with a registered dietitian who specializes in sports nutrition.

Steps to Resolve Eating Disorders

If you are spending too much time obsessing about food, weight and exercise, seek help and information by contacting:

National Eating Disorders Association (information and referral network)
www.NationalEatingDisorders.org

American Dietetic Association (referral network)
www.eatright.org

Something Fishy Website on Eating Disorders (information and referral network)
www.something-fishy.org

Gurze Books (recommended self-help books)
www.bulimia.com

If you suspect your training partner or friend is struggling with food issues, speak up! Anorexia and bulimia are self-destructive eating behaviors that may signal underlying depression and can be life-threatening. Here are some helpful tips:

- Approach the person gently but be persistent. Say that you are worried about her health. She, too, may be concerned about her loss of concentration, light-headedness, or chronic fatigue. These health changes are more likely to be a stepping stone to accepting help, since the person clings to food and exercise for feelings of control and stability.
- Don't discuss weight or eating habits. Address the fundamental problems of life. Focus on unhappiness as the reason for seeking help. Point out how anxious, tired, and/or irritable the person has been lately. Emphasize that she doesn't have to be that way.
- Post a list of resources (with tear-off websites at the bottom) where the person will see it (see resources listed above).

Remember that you are not responsible and can only try to help. Your power comes from using community resources and health professionals, such as a counselor, nutritionist, or eating disorders clinic.

The following tips may help you resume menses or at least rule out nutrition-related factors.

1. *Throw away the bathroom scale.* Rather than striving to achieve a certain number on the scale, let your body weigh what it weighs. Focus on how healthy you feel and how well you perform, rather than on the number you weigh.
2. *If you have weight to lose, don't crash-diet* but rather moderately cut back on your food intake by about 20 percent. Severe dieters commonly lose their menstrual periods, suggesting that amenorrhea may be an adaptation to the calorie deficit produced either by low calorie intake alone or by increased energy expenditure via exercise. In particular, rapid weight loss may predispose you to amenorrhea. By following a healthy reducing program, as outlined in Chapter 15, you'll not only have greater success with long-term weight loss, but also have enough energy to run.
3. *If you are at an appropriate weight, practice eating as you did as a child:* Eat when you are hungry, stop when you are content. If you are always hungry and constantly obsessing about food, you are undoubtedly trying to eat too few calories. Chapter 14 can help you determine an appropriate calorie intake and eating schedule that may differ from your current routine, particularly if you yo-yo between starving and bingeing.
4. *Eat adequate protein.* Research has suggested that amenorrheic runners tend to eat less protein than their regularly menstruating counterparts. In one study, 82 percent of the amenorrheic women ate less than the recommended dietary allowance for protein. Even if you are a vegetarian, remember that you still need adequate protein (see Chapter 6).
5. *Eat at least 20 percent of your calories from fat.* Amenorrheic marathoners commonly are afraid of eating fat. They think that if they eat fat, they'll get fat. Although excess calories from fat are easily fattening, some fat (20 to 30 percent of total calories) is an appropriate part of a healthy sports diet. For most active people, this translates into about 40 to 60 or more grams of fat per day. Clearly, this differs from a no-fat diet and allows lean meats, peanut butter, nuts, olive oil, and other wholesome foods and healthful fats that balance a sports diet (see Chapter 7).
6. *Maintain a calcium-rich diet.* You should choose a high-calcium diet to help maintain bone density. Because you build peak bone density in your teens and early adult years, your goal is to protect against future problems with osteoporosis by eating calcium-rich foods today. As I mentioned in Chapter 1, a safe target is at least 1,000 milligrams of calcium per day if you are between nineteen and fifty years old, and 1,200 to 1,300 milligrams of calcium per day if you are amenorrheic or post-menopausal. This is the equivalent to including a serving of milk, yogurt, and other dairy or calcium-rich foods at each meal in the day.

Chapter 1 provides guidelines for getting an optimal amount of calcium. Although you may cringe at the thought of spending so many calories on dairy foods, remember that milk is not an "optional fluid" but rather a wholesome food that contains many important nutrients. Some research also suggests women who consume three or more glasses of milk or yogurt per day tend to be leaner than those who do not consume as much dairy.

Calcium is only one factor that affects bone density. There is a genetic factor to osteoporosis; if your mother or grandmother has/had osteoporosis, you are more likely to get the disease. Other factors that contribute to your risk for osteoporosis include being too thin, getting inadequate exercise, and having low levels of estrogen. Because you are athletic, your bones benefit from the protective effect of exercise, particularly strength training. But exercise does not override the health dangers of being too thin, consuming inadequate calcium or lacking estrogen (as occurs with amenorrhea).

Summary

Food should be one of life's pleasures, a fun part of your marathon training program, and a protector of your good health. If you spend too much time thinking about food as being a fattening enemy, I highly recommend you consult a registered dietitian who specializes in sports nutrition and eating disorders (use the referral network at www.eatright.org). This professional can help you transform your food fears into healthful fueling so your body can support your goals of training for and completing the marathon in good health, with high energy, and finding peace with food and your body.

Muesli

Muesli is a standard breakfast in Europe, and it can also be eaten for lunch or a light supper. It's a cook-free combination of dairy, fruit and whole grains that can bolster your health and energy. For dieters, muesli is a good way to start your day with a portfolio of wholesome foods.

1/2 cup (40 g) oats (regular or quick-cooking)
1/2 cup (115 g) plain yogurt, preferably low-fat
1 tablespoon (15 g) lemon juice
1 small apple, grated
1 small banana, sliced
3 tablespoons (30 g) raisins
honey or sugar to taste

Optional:
- chopped nuts (walnuts, almonds, hazelnuts)
- berries (strawberries, blueberrires, blackberries, raspberries)
- sliced peaches, apricots or pears

1. In a large bowl, combine the oats and yogurt. Add the lemon juice and the grated apples. Mix immediately to avoid discoloration of the apples.
2. Add the bananas and raisins, and any of the optional ingredients.
3. Sweeten to taste with sugar or honey.

Yield: 1 serving
Total calories: 450
Carbohydrates: 95 grams, Protein: 12, Fat: 3

RECIPE

Chapter 17

How to Gain Weight Healthfully

> "When I started to train for the marathon, I was too busy to eat. I lost weight and felt self-conscious about my scrawny legs and skinny body. I contemplated quitting the training program, because I was afraid I'd turn into a bag of bones. Instead, I made an effort to better plan my sports diet. I started drinking lots more juice and milk, and having a peanut butter and honey sandwich before bed."

*Justin Holmes,
Wellesley MA*

If you are among the minority of marathoners who struggles with being too thin, food may seem a medicine, meals a burden, and food shopping a budget-breaker. Gaining weight is hard work! Through strength training and diet, you can change your physique to a certain extent, but first, be sure you have a realistic goal based on your genetic blueprint:

- What do other people in your family look like?
- Was your mother or father very slim at your age?
- When did he or she gain weight?
- What does he or she look like now?

If, at your age, a parent was similarly thin, you probably are genetically predisposed to being thin and may have trouble adding pounds. Some people are simply "hard gainers." For example, in an overfeeding study on identical twins, some pairs of twins gained more weight than others, despite the fact that everyone over-ate by an equal amount—1,000 extra calories per day (Bouchard, 1990). In another study, some subjects who theoretically should have gained eleven pounds during a month-long overfeeding study gained an average of only six pounds. Why the difference? Perhaps the "hard gainers" fidgeted more than others; fidgeting can burn an extra 300 to 700 calories per day! In comparison, "easy gainers" tend to enjoy sitting calmly.

Six Rules for Gaining Weight

If you are a hard gainer, you can try to fidget less (unlikely!) and consume more calories than you expend. Adding muscle-building exercise, such as weightlifting, helps convert the extra calories into muscle rather than fat.

I encourage underweight marathoners to consume an additional 500 to 1,000 calories per day. If you are committed to the weight-gain process, you can expect to gain one-half to one pound per week, perhaps more depending on your age. For example, high school and collegiate athletes may bulk-up more easily than the fully mature 35-year-old who is genetically skinny.

The trick to successful weight gain is to pay careful attention to these six important rules.

1. *Eat consistently.* Have at least three or four hearty meals plus one or two additional snacks daily. Do not skip meals! You may not feel hungry for lunch if you've had a big breakfast, but you should eat regardless. Otherwise, you'll miss out on important calories that you need to accomplish your goal.

2. *Eat larger portions.* Some people think they need to buy expensive weight-gain powders. They don't need special powders; standard food works fine. The only reason commercial powders "work" is because they provide additional calories.

For example, one marathoner religiously drank the recommended three glasses per day of a 300-calorie weight-gain shake. This gave him an extra 900 calories and the desired results. Although he credited the weight-gain formula for his success, he could have less expensively consumed those calories with supermarket foods. I suggested that he invest his food budget in readily available foods:

- a bigger bowl of cereal
- a larger piece of fruit
- an extra sandwich for lunch or a large sub sandwich
- three potatoes at dinner instead of two
- a taller glass of milk.

When he did this, he met his goal of 1,000 extra calories per day and continued to see the desired results.

3. *Select higher calorie foods, but not higher fat foods.* Excess fat calories easily convert into body fat that fattens you up rather than bulks up your muscles. The best bet for extra calories is to choose carbohydrate-dense foods that have more calories than an equally enjoyable counterpart (see sidebar, How to Boost Your Calories). These extra carbohydrates will give you the energy you need to do muscle-building exercise. By reading food labels, you'll be able to make the best choices.

How to Boost Your Calories

Choose more:	Calories	Amount	Instead of:	Calories	Amount
Cranberry juice	170	8 oz (240 ml)	Orange juice	110	8 ounces
Grape juice	160	8 oz (240 ml)	Grapefruit juice	100	8 ounces
Banana	170	1 large	Apple	130	1 large
Granola	780	1.5 cups (150 g)	Bran flakes	200	1.5 cups (60 g)
Grape-Nuts	660	1.5 cups (175)	Cheerios	160	1.5 cups (45 g)
Corn	140	1 cup (165 g)	Green beans	40	1 cup (120 g)
Carrots	45	1 cup (150 g)	Zucchini	30	1 cup (180 g)
Split pea soup	130	1 cup (240 ml)	Vegetable soup	80	1 cup
Baked beans	260	1 cup (260 g)	Rice	190	1 cup (160 g)

4. *Drink lots of juice and low-fat milk.* Beverages are a simple way to increase your calorie intake. Replace part or all of the water you drink with calorie-containing fluids. One high school athlete gained 13 pounds over the summer by simply subtracting water and adding six glasses of cranapple juice (about 1,000 calories) to his standard daily diet. Extra juices are not only a great source of calories and fluids but also of carbohydrates to keep your muscles well fueled.

5. *Do strength training (push-ups, weightlifting) to stimulate muscular development so that you bulk up instead of fatten up.* Note that extra exercise, not extra protein, is the key to muscular development. One skinny marathoner expressed concern the extra exercise would result in weight loss rather than weight gain. I reminded him that exercise tends to stimulate the appetite. Yes, a hard run may temporarily "kill" your appetite right after the workout because your body temperature is elevated, but within a few hours when you have cooled down, you will be plenty hungry. The more you exercise, the more you'll want to eat—assuming you make the time to do so.

6. *Be patient.* If you are in high school or college and don't easily bulk-up this year, you may do so more easily as you get older. Know that you can be a strong marathoner by being well fueled and well trained. Your skinny legs may hurt your self-esteem more than your athletic ability.

Apple Brown Betty

This is a yummy way to boost your intake of calories, as well as your intake fruit and carbs. A wholesome dessert for a hungry marathoner.

11 sheets (1/3 box; 340 g) graham crackers
1/4 cup (60 g) soft margarine, melted
6 large (1.2 kg) apples, unpeeled
3/4 cup (145 g) brown sugar
1 teaspoon (4 g) cinnamon
1/2 cup (120 ml) water
Optional: 1/4 tsp. (1 g) nutmeg
1/4 tsp (1 g) cloves
2 tablespoons (30 ml) lemon juice
1/2 cup (70 g) raisins and/or chopped nuts

- Crush the graham crackers into crumbs by placing them in a plastic bag and rolling them with a rolling pin or a bottle.
- In a bowl, combine the crumbs with the melted margarine.
- Put one-third of the mixture in the bottom of a 2-quart (2-liter) casserole dish.
- Core and slice the apples into thin wedges and put them into a bowl. Sprinkle the apple wedges with sugar, cinnamon, and other spices, as well as lemon juice, as desired.
- Put the apple slices into the baking dish; add 1/2 cup water and then the rest of the graham cracker crumbs.
- Cover and bake at 350° F (175° C) for 25 minutes; uncover, then bake another 15 minutes to crispen.

Total calories: 2,500
8 servings
Calories per serving: 310

Afterword

Training for a marathon is big commitment. It consumes hours of your time and drains both your mental and physical energy. Yet, the process is exciting, rewarding, and hopefully, enjoyable. If you are participating in the marathon as a part of a fundraising effort, you will gain the additional satisfaction associated with helping make a difference in the world.

I hope this book helps you enjoy your months of preparation, as well as the 26.2-mile event itself. During this process, you'll learn a lot about your body and your strenghts, both mental and physical. You'll learn what foods work and what ones don't. You'll likely be nervous and anxious as the day draws closer. As one first-time marathoner asked me with wringing hands, "Is running a marathon, well, worse than childbirth?" I assured her that completing a marathon can be far less painful; it can even be fun!

You've read the tricks on how to keep yourself well fueled and appropriately hydrated. I now wish you the best for your efforts. Have a good one!

Nancy Clark

Additional Resources

To find a local sports nutritionist contact:

American Dietetic Association
P.O. Box 97215
Chicago, IL 60678
Tel.: (800) 366-1655
Or, use their convenient referral network at *www.eatright.org* and *www.SCANdpg.org*

Newsletters

Tufts University Health & Nutrition Letter
P.O. Box 420235
Palm Coast, FL 32142-0235
Tel.: (800) 274-7581
http://healthletter.tufts.edu

University of California at Berkeley Wellness Letter
P.O. Box 42018
Palm Coast, FL 32142
Tel.: (386) 447-6328
www.berkeleywellness.com

Catalogs for nutrition books and other resources

Nutrition topics

Nutrition Counseling and Education Services
1904 East 123rd Street
Olathe, KS 66061
Tel.: (888) 545-5653
www.ncescatalog.com

Eating disorders

Gurze Books
P.O. Box 2238
Carlsbad, CA 92018
Tel.: (800) 756-7533
www.gurze.net

Fitness and sports nutrition

Human Kinetics
P.O. Box 5076
Champaign, Illinois 61825-5076
Tel.: (800) 747-4457
www.humankinetics.com

Recommended Books

Benardot, Dan. *Advanced Sports Nutrition*. Human Kinetics, 2006.
Clark, Nancy. *Nancy Clark's Sports Nutrition Guidebook,* Third Edition. Human Kinetics, 2003.
Clark, Nancy. *The Cyclist's Food Guide: Fueling for the Distance*. www.nancyclarkrd.com, 2005.
Colberg, Sheri. *The Diabetic Athlete*. Human Kinetics, 2001.
Duyff, Roberta. *The American Dietetic Association's Complete Food and Nutrition Guide*. Chronimed Publishing, 2006.
Freedman, Rita. *BodyLove: Learning to Like Our Looks and Ourselves*. Gurze Books, 2002.
Heffner, M. The Anorexia Workbook: *How to accept yourself, heal your suffering & reclaim your life*, 2004.
Hirschmann, Jane and Carol Munter. *When Women Stop Hating Their Bodies: Freeing Yourself from Food and Weight Obsession*. Fawcett Books, 1997.
Larsen-Meyer, Enette. *Vegetarian Sports Nutrition*. Human Kinetics, 2006
LoBue, Andrea and Marsea Marcus. *The Don't Diet, Live-It! Workbook: Healing Food, Weight & Body Issues*. Gurze Books, 1999.
McCabe, Randi and Traci McFarlane. *The Overcoming Bulimia Workbook*. Gurze Books, 2003
Satter, Ellyn. *Secrets of Feeding a Healthy Family*. Kelcy Press, 1999.
Satter, Ellyn. *Your Overweight Child: Helping Without Harming,* Kelcy Press, 2005.
Siegel, Michelle, Judith Brisman, and Margot Weinshel. *Surviving an Eating Disorder: Strategies for Families and Friends*. HarperCollins, 1997.
Tribole, Evelyn and Elyse Resch. *Intuitive Eating: A revolutionary program that works*. St. Martins Press, 2003.

For Coaches and Professionals

Dunford, Marie Ed. *Sports Nutrition: A Guide for the Professional Working with Active People,* fourth edition. American Dietetics Association, 2005.

Internet Resources

Sports and Sports Nutrition

Nancy Clark, MS, RD
www.nancyclarkrd.com
Links to nutrition articles and other nutrition sources; information on teaching materials

Australian Institute of Sport
www.ais.org.au/nutrition
Comprehensive information on physical fitness and nutrition

Gatorade Sports Science Institute
www.gssiweb.com
Information on endurance sports nutrition

Sportscience
www.sportsci.org
An interdisciplinary site for research on human physical performance

WaddleOn.com
www.waddleon.com
An Internet guide to becoming an athlete, whatever your size or shape

Health and Nutrition

ConsumerLab.com
www.consumerlab.com
Independently tests nutritional supplements and posts the results

International Food Information Council Foundation
http://ific.org
Geared mostly toward health professionals, the site features information on food safety and nutrition

National Library of Medicine, U.S. Department of Health and Human Services
www.nlm.nih.gov
Free access to medical journals

U.S. Department of Health and Human Services
www.healthfinder.gov
Provides information and lists publications and not-for-profit organizations that produce reliable information

Eating disorders

National Eating Disorders Association
www.NationalEatingDisorders.org
Information, resources, and links for eating disorders

Something Fishy Website on Eating Disorders
www.something-fishy.org
Offers extensive resources and referrals for eating disorders.

Selected References

American Dietetic Association, American College of Sports Medicine, and Dietitians of Canada. "Joint Position Statement: Nutrition and Athletic Performance." *Journal of the American Dietetic Association.* 12: 1543–56, 2000.

Association of International Marathon Medical Directors Statement on Fluids. http://www.medicalnewstoday.com/medicalnews.php?newsis = 50087

Berardi, J., T. Price, E. Noreen and P. Lemon. "Postexercise Muscle Glycogen Recovery Enhanced with a Carbohydrate-Protein Supplement." *Med Sci Sports Exerc 38,* (6):1106-1113, 2006.

Beals, K. and M. Manore. "Behavioral, Psychological, and Physical Characteristics of Female Athletes with Subclinical Eating Disorders." *International Journal of Sports Nutrition and Exercise Metabolism.* 10, (2):128–43, 2000.

Brouns, F., W. Saris, and N. Rehrer. "Abdominal Complaints and Gastro-Intestinal Function During Long-Lasting Exercise." *International Journal of Sports Medicine.* 8 :175–89, 1987.

Bouchard, C., et al. "The Response to Long Term Overfeeding in Identical Twins." *New England Journal of Medicine.* 322:1477–82, 1990.

Burke, L. "Nutritional Needs for Exercise in the Heat." *Comparative Biochemistry and Physiology Part* A 128, no. 4:735–48, 2001.

Carrithers, J.A., et al. "Effects of Post-Exercise Protein-Carbohydrate Feedings on Muscle Glycogen Restoration." *Journal of Applied Physiology.* 88, no. 6:1976–82, 2000.

Casa, D., et al. "National Athletic Trainers' Association Position Statement: Fluid Replacement for Athletes." *Journal of Athletic Training.* 35, no. 2: 212–24, 2000.

Clark, N., M. Nelson, and W. Evans. "Nutrition Education for Elite Women Runners." *Physician and Sportsmedicine.* 16 (2): 124–34, 1988.

Garner, D. "The Effects of Starvation on Behavior: Implications for Dieting and Eating Disorders." *Healthy Weight Journal.* 12 (5): 68–72, 1998.

Hagberg, J., et al. "Determinants of Body Composition in Post-Menopausal Women." *Journal of Gerontology.* Series A—Biol Sci Med Sci 55 (10): M607–12, 2000.

Hill, R.J. and P.S. Davies. "The Validity of Self-Reported Energy Intake as Determined Using the Doubly Labeled Water Technique." *British Journal of Nutrition.* 85 (4): 415–30, 2001.

Ivy, J. H. Goforth, B. Damon, T. McCauley, E. Parsons, and T. Price. "Early post-exercise muscle glycogen recovery is enhanced with a carbohdyrate-protein supplement." *J Appl Physiol* 93(4):1337-1344, 2002.

Jakicic, J., et al. "American College of Sports Medicine Position Stand. Appropriate Intervention Strategies for Weight Loss and Prevention of Weight Regain for Adults." *Medicine and Science in Sports and Exercise.* 12: 2145–56, 2001.

Lichtenstein, A. et al. "Diet and Lifestyle Recommendation Revision 2006: A Scientific Statement From the American Heart Association Nutrition Committee." *Circulation* 2006; 114:82-96, 2006.

Malcsewska, J., G. Raczynski, and R. Stupnicki. "Iron Status in Female Endurance Athletes and Non-Athletes." *International Journal of Sports Nutrition and Exercise Metabolism.* 10 (3): 260–76, 2000.

Nativ, A. "Stress Fractures and Bone Health in Track and Field Athletes." *Journal of Science and Medicine in Sport.* 3 (3):268–79, 2000.

Pedersen, A., et al. "Menstrual Differences Due to Vegetarian and Non-Vegetarian Diets." *American Journal of Clinical Nutrition.* 53: 879–85, 1991.

Pendergast, D., J. Leddy, and J. Veentkatraman. "A Perspective on Fat Intake in Athletes." *Journal of the American College of Nutrition.* 19 (3): 345–50, 2000.

Rehrer, N. "Fluid and Electrolyte Balance in Ultra-Endurance Sport." *Sports Medicine.* 31 (10): 701–15, 2001.

Sanborn, C.F., B. Albrecht, and W. Wagner. "Athletic Amenorrhea: Lack of Association with Body Fat." *Medicine and Science in Sports and Exercise.* 19 (3): 207–12, 1987.

Sanborn, C.F., et al. "Disordered Eating and the Female Athlete Triad." *Clinical Sports Medicine.* 19 (2): 199–213, 2000.

Schulz, L.O., et al. "Energy Expenditure of Elite Female Runners Measured by Respiratory Chamber and Doubly Labeled Water." *Journal of Applied Physiology.* 72 (1): 23–28, 1992.

Sherman, W.M. "Muscle Glycogen Supercompensation During the Week Before Athletic Competition." *Sports Science Exchange* (The Gatorade Institute). 2 (16): 1989.

Wilmore, J., et al. "Is There Energy Conservation in Amenorrheic Compared with Eumenorrheic Distance Runners?" *Journal of Applied Physiology.* 72 (1): 15–22, 1992.

Wyatt, HR et al. "Long-term weight loss and breakfast in subjects in the National Weight Control Registry." *Obes Research.* 10(2)78-82, 2002.

Zelasko, C. "Exercise for Weight Loss: What Are the Facts?" *Journal of the American Dietetic Association.* 95:1414–17, 1995.

Index

Alcoholic beverages: 11, 109
     fluid replacement with 109
     as recovery fluid 102
Amenorrhea: 139-144
     causes of, ...140
     definition of, ...139
     and health risks, ...140
     resolving, ...140-144
     risk factors for, ...143
     and a vegetarian diet, ...143
American College of Sports Medicine 76
American Dietetic Association, ...16, 142, 150
     See also Dietitians
American Heart Association, ...11
Amino Acids. *See* Protein
Anemia, iron-deficiency: 45, 60
     and fatigue, ...45
     prevention of, ...45
     See also Iron
Animal fats. *See* Fats, dietary
Anorexia. *See* Eating disorders
Antioxidants. *See* Vitamins, anti-oxidant
Appetite:
     controlling, ...124, 130
     morning, ...23, 24, 30
     natural, ...122, 124
     post-exercise, ...99
     on weight reduction diet, ...122-124
Ascorbic acid. *See* Vitamin C

Balanced diet, ...10
Banana Bread, ...27 (recipe)
Bananas:
     carbohydrate in, ...51
     -recipes with: Banana Bread, ...27
Beans, dried (legumes):
     as iron source, ...59, 62 (table)
     as protein source, ...59 (table), 60
     serving suggestions for, ...60-61
     -recipes with: Hummus, ...56
Beef. *See* Meat
Beer, ...78 (table), 109
     See also alcoholic beverages

Beverages: 76-80
        pre-exercise, ...87
        See also Alcoholic beverages; Fluids; Water
        recipes for: Homemade Sports Drink, ...80
Blood glucose. *See* Blood sugar
Blood pressure. *See* Hypertension
Blood sugar:
        low (hypoglycemia), ...44, 52, 84, 90
        See also Glycemic effect of foods
Body fat: 128, 133
        and amenorrhea, ...140, 143
        burning versus losing, ...131
        essential, ...138
        gender differences in, ...138
Body image, ...134, 138-139
Bone density, ...143
Bones:
        and osteoporosis, ...43, 140
        stress fractures, ...143
Bonking. *See* "Hitting the wall"
Bowel movements, ...112
        See also Constipation; Diarrhea; Fiber; Digestion; Stomach
Bran cereals, ...24
        See also Fiber
Breads:
        as protein source, ...59 (table)
        See also Carbohydrates; Grains and starches
        recipe for: Banana Bread, ...27
Breakfast: 20-27
        balanced, ...24
        digesting, ...23
        as dining-out meal, ...116, 119
        for early-morning exercisers, ...23
        as most important meal of day, ...22
        non-traditional, ...25
        pre-event or pre-exercise, ...84, 109
        recipes for, ...144
        as recovery meal, ...23
        skipping, ...22
        suggestions for, ...26 (table), 103, 109
        See also Breads; Breakfast cereals
Breakfast cereals:
        choosing, ...24-26, 43
        fat in, ...26
        fiber-rich, ...24-25
        as iron source, ...25

     as protein source, ...59 (table)
     suggestions for, ...144
     when traveling, ...116
     recipe with: Breakfast for Travelers, ...119
Brown rice. *See* Rice
Budgeting calories. *See* Calories, daily budgeting of
Bulimia. *See* Eating Disorders

Caffeine: 87
     See also Coffee
Calcium:
     and amenorrhea, ...143
     and osteoporosis, ...143
     recommended intake of, ...11, 14, 16 (table), 143
     sources of, ...10 (table)
Calculating calorie needs. *See* Calories, estimating need for
Calories: 120-125
     counting, ...122
     daily budgeting of, ...120-125
     daily intake of, ...124
     estimating need for, ...122-123
     need for during exercise, ...84
     over-restricting, ...130
     See also Weight-gain diet; Weight-reduction diet
Candy. *See* Sweets
Carbohydrate loading: 104-111
     fluids required during, ...92-93, 109
     sample carbo-loading menu, ...110-111, 113
     versus fat-loading, ...107
     and weight gain, ...50, 107
Carbohydrates: 48-54
     athletes' need for, ...12,50, 54, 106
     caloric content of, ...50
     complex (starches), ...51
     during exercise, ...77
     as fundamental nutrient, ...12, 50
     not fattening, ...50
     pre-exercise, ...87
     as recovery food, ...97-98
     simple, ...51
     sources of, ...10 (table), 51, 87 (table)
     in sports drinks, ...77
     target intake of, ...106-107
     and weight gain, ...50
     See also Glycemic effect of a food
Cereals. *See* Breakfast cereals

Chicken:
     cooking tips for, ...62
     as example of muscle fiber types, ...64
     fat in, ...78 (table)
     as iron source, ...62 (table)
     as protein source, ...58 (table)
     as zinc source, ...63 (table)
     -recipe with: Mexican Baked Chicken with Beans, ...39
Chicken, Mexican Baked with Beans, ...39 (recipe)
Cholesterol, blood, ...51
Cholesterol, in meat, ...51
Coffee, ...87, 112
     See also Caffeine
Commercial sports foods, ...92-93, 100
Constipation, ...107, 112
     See also Bowel movements; Fiber
Crash dieting, ...129, 143
Cravings. *See* Food cravings

Dairy products:
     fat in, ...69 (table)
     nutritional value of, ...16 (table)
     as protein source, ...59 (table)
     See also Calcium, sources of
Dehydration, prevention of, ...76-79, 90
     See also Fluids; Sweating; Water
Dessert,
     See also Sugar; Junk foods
     recipe for: . . . . .148 (Apple Brown Betty)
Diarrhea, ...26, 82, 95
     See also Bowel movements; Stomach
Diet:
     balance and variety in, ...10-15
     low-carbohydrate, ...44
     low-fat, ...68-69
     vegetarian, ...58-59, 66, 143
     for weight reduction, ...130-134
     See also Weight-gain diet; Weight-reduction diet
Dietitians, ...16
Digestion:
     before and during exercise, ...23, 82-85
     of liquid versus solid food, ...85
     of pre-exercise meals (*See* Eating, pre-exercise)
     of energy bars, ...92
     See also Meals; Eating
Dining out. *See* Breakfast; Dinner; Fast foods; Lunch

Dinner: 34-38
       as dining-out meal, ...118
       suggestions for simple, ...34-39
Double workouts, ...99
Dressings, for salads. *See* Salad dressing
Drinking, programmed, ...90
       See also Fluids

Eating:
       after exercise, ...97-103
       during exercise, .89-96, 112. 117, 131
       pre-exercise, ...81-82, 86
       pre-marathon, ...104-113, 117
       programmed, ...10
       timing of, ...131
       See also Diet; Digestion; Fast foods; Liquid meals,
       pre-competition; Meals; Snacking
Eating disorders: 136-144
       helping someone with, ...142
       professional resources for, ...142, 151
Electrolytes, ...77
Endurance. *See* Carbohydrate loading
Energy bars, ...93
       Homemade, ...96 (recipe)
Energy Bar, Honey Crisp. . . . . .96 (recipe)
Energy efficiency, ...139, 141
Exercise:
       caloric expenditure with, ...123, 124
       early-morning, ...84
       See also Eating; Fluids
Exercise intensity, ...83

Fast foods: 31
       fat and calories in, ...70 (table), 118
       See also Junk food; Dining out
Fast-twitch muscle fibers. *See* Muscle fiber types
Fat, body. *See* Body fat
Fatigue, possible causes of, ...44-46
Fats, dietary: 67-72
       and amenorrhea, ...143
       choices of, ...68
       cutting down on, ...11
       fear of, ...72, 143
       in fish, ...43
       in foods, ...69 (table)
       as a fundamental nutrient, ...72

     healthful, ...68, 72

     pre-exercise, ...118

     saturated, ...72

     target intake of, ...15, 68 (table), 132

     in weight-gain diet, ...147

     in weight-reduction diet, ...68, 132

     See also Oils

Fiber:

     in cereals, ...25, 26 (table)

     See also Breakfast Cereals; Grains and starches

Fish:

     buying and cooking of, ...65

     fat in, ...43

     highest in fish oils, ...64

     mercury in, ...64

     as protein source, ...59 (table), 63

     recipe with: Fish Florentine, ...66

Fish Florentine, ...66 (recipe)

Fish oil, ...43, 46, 68

Fluids: 74-80

     comparing, ...78 (table), 100

     during exercise, ...79, 117

     lost with sweating, ...76

     myths about, ...79

     pre-event, ...77

     post-exercise, ...99

     pre-exercise, ...77

     replacing sweat losses of, ...76

     sodium in, ...78 (table)

     See also Beverages; Dehydration; Drinking, programmed;

     Sports drinks; Water

Food cravings: 51

     for salt, ...79

     for sweets, ...51

Food, pre-exercise. *See* Eating, pre-exercise

Food record (diary), ...130

Food groups, ...12

Fruit:

     nutritional value of, ...10

     recommneded intake, ...13

     recipes with: Apple Brown Betty, ...148

Fruit juice: 116

     for boosting calorie intake, ...147

     carbohydrates in, ...116 (table)

     as potassium source, ...118 (table)

     as recovery fluid, ...100

Fuel for exercise. *See* Eating

Gain weight. *See* Weight Gain

Galloway, Jeff, ... 7

Gastrointestinal (GI) problems. See Digestion

Gatorade, ... 78 (table), 92, 100

        See also Sports drinks

Gels, ...93

Glycemic effect of a food, ...52

Glycogen, ...45

Grains and starches: 10

        as iron source, ...62 (table)

        as protein source, ...58 (table),

        See also Breakfast cereals; Pasta; Potatoes and sweet potatoes; Rice

Heart disease, and fat, ...43, 59 (table)

        See also Cholesterol; Diet, Fat, dietary

Hitting the wall, ...106

Homemade Sports Drink, ...80 (recipe)

Hummus, ... 56 (recipe)

Hunger. *See* Appetite

Hydration. *See* Dehydration; Fluids

Hypoglycemia (low blood sugar). *See* Blood sugar, low

Hyponatremia, ...78

Iron:

        absorption of, ...66

        boosting intake of, ...25, 45, 62 (table)

        deficiency of, ...43, 45, 60

        requirements for, ...62 (table)

        sources of, ...25, 62 (table)

        See also Anemia, iron-deficiency; Meat, and anemia

Juices. *See* Fruit juice

Junk food, ...10, 15

        See also Desserts; Sugar; Snack foods

Lactose, intolerance to, ...14

Lasagna, Easy, ...113 (recipe)

Legumes. *See* Beans, dried (legumes)

Liquid meals, pre-competition, ...85

Liver glycogen, ...84

Low blood sugar. *See* Blood sugar, low

Low-fat diet, ...68

Lunch: 30-32

        as dining-out meal, ...116

        brown-bag, ...30

        fast-food, ...31

        suggestions for, ...30-31

Marathon day: 106-113
        nutritional mistakes on, ...106-109
        breakfast, ...117
        carbohydrate loading for, ...106-113

Meals:
        liquid, ...85
        pre-exercise, ...86, 106
        suggestions for simple, .36, 52, 86
        timing of, ...87, 131
        See also Breakfast; Dinner; Eating; Lunch

Meat:
        and amenorrhea, ...63, 143
        and anemia, ...62
        and cholesterol, ...61
        fat in, ...61, 66, 69 (table)
        hormones in, ...63
        as iron source, ...61
        and protein, ...59
        as zinc source, ...62

Meatless diet. *See* Diet, vegetarian
Meatless entrees, ...60
        See also Beans, dried (legumes); Fish

Menstruation: 139-149
        lack of. *See* Amenorrhea
        and red meat, ...143

Metabolic rate, ...122
Metabolism, slow, ...129, 139

Milk:
        fat in, ...64 (table)
        as protein source, ...14, 59 (table)
        See also Dairy products; Calcium

Mind, power of, ...87
Muscle fiber types, ...64
Muscle fuel. *See* Glycogen; Muscle glycogen

Muscle glycogen:
        replenishing after exercise, ...98-103
        weight gain from, ...107

National Eating Disorders Association, .142
Nausea post-exercice, ...102
Nutrition, post-exercise. *See* Recovery foods; Eating, after exercise
Nutrition, pre-exercise. *See* Eating, pre-exercise; Meals
Nutritionists. *See* Dietitians

Oatmeal:
      recipes with: Breakfast for Travelers,
      See also Breakfast cereals
Oils: 68
      fat in, ...70 (table)
      See also Fat, dietary; Salad dressing
Omega-three fatty acids. See Fish, fat in
Osteoporosis, ...140
Oven Fries, ...73 (recipe)
Overeating, ...51
Overtraining, ...45
Overweight. *See* Weight-reduction diet

Pancakes, Power, ...103 (recipe)
Pasta: 53
      cooking tips for, ...53
      as protein source, ...37 (table)
      serving suggestions for, .55 (table)
Peas, dried. *See* Beans, dried (legumes)
Perspiration. *See* Sweating
Phytochemicals, ...43
Pork. *See* Meat
Potassium:
      in fluid replacers, ...78 (table)
      losses in sweat, ... 78 (table)
Potatoes and sweet potatoes:
      carbohydrates in, ...55
      cooking tips for, ...55
      in dining-out meals, ...118
      serving suggestions for, ...55
      recipe with: Oven French Fries, ...73
Poultry. *See* Chicken
Pre-exercise meals, ...84-87
      See also Eating, pre-exercise; pre-competition; Meals
Protein: 57-66
      and amenorrhea, ...143
      bars, ...65, 66, 94
      deficiency of, ...58, 60, 143
      for endurance athletes, ...58
      as fundamental nutrient, ...58
      recommended intake of, ...13 (table), 58, 59 (table)
      as recovery food, ...101-103
      sources of, ...10 (table), 50 (table), 59 (table)
      vegetarian sources for, ...50
      in weight-gain diet, ...148
      in weight-reduction diet, ...50

Protein Bars, ...94
Protein shakes. *See* Shakes, for weight gain
Protein supplements, ...58, 64

Recipes:
    Apple Brown Betty. 148
    Banana Bread, ... 27
    Banana Frostie, ...125
    Breakfast for Travellers, .119
    Chicken, Mexican Baked with Beans, ...38
    Energy Bar, Honey Crisp, .96
    Fish Florentine, ...66
    Greek Salad, Brenda's, ...135
    Hummus, ...56
    Lasagna, Easy 113
    Muesli, ...144
    Oven French Fries, ...72
    Power Pancakes, ...102
    Sports Drink, Homemade, ...80
    Sugar and Spice Trail Mix, ...88
    Super Salad, ...47
    Vegetables, ...17-18
Recovery fluids, ...98-99, 101 (table)
    See also Fluids; Water
Recovery foods: 97-103, 117
    popular, ...101 (table)
    potassium in, ...78 (table)
    protein as, ...101-102
    sodium in, .78-79, 100-102
    See also Eating, after exercise
Recovery, time for, ...23, 103
Reducing diet. *See* Weight-reduction diet
Restaurant meals. *See* Dining out; Fast foods; Traveling
Resting metabolic rate, .122-123
Rice:
    cooking tips for, ...35, 54
    meal ideas, ...35, 54

Salad bars, ...32
Salad dressing:
    calories in, ...32
    in dining-out meals, ...118
Salads:
    comparing fixings for, ...32 (table)
    suggestions for, ...47 (recipe), 118

Salt:

    cravings for, ...79, 101

    and high blood pressure, ...26, 36

    need for extra, ...78, 101

    replacing sweat losses of, ... 78

    in sweat, ...78 (table),

Sandwiches, suggestions for, ...30-31

Serum cholesterol: *See* Cholesterol, blood

Shakes, for weight gain, ...147

Shopping, food, ...35 (table)

Slow-twitch muscle fibers, ...64

Snack foods:

    fat in, ...71 (table)

    outrageous, ...34

    portable, ...33

    suggestions for, ... 33 (table), 91 (table), 119

    See also Fast food; Junk food

Snacking:

    controlling hunger by, ...30, 131

    during exercise, ...91 (table)

    planning for, ... 33

    pre-exercise (See Eating, pre-exercise)

    from vending machine, ...34

    See also Snack foods

Sodium:

    during extended exercise, ...77

    in fluid replacers, ...78 (table)

    and high blood pressure, ...26, 36

    in recovery foods, ...78 (table), 110

    in sports drinks, ... 78 (table)

    See also Salt

Soft drinks: 100, 118

    during exercise, ...79

    as recovery fluid, ...99, 101 (table), 117

SomethingFishy Website, ...142

Soups:

    suggestions for, ...36, 118

    in dining-out meals, ...118

Spaghetti. *See* Pasta

Sports bars. *See* Energy bars

Sports Drink, Homemade, ...80 (recipe)

Sports drinks: 77-78, 92

    electrolytes in, ...78 (table)

    during exercise, ...77, 100

    carbohydrates in, ...77

    ingredients in, ...80

need for, ...77, 90

potassium in, ...78 (table)

as recovery fluid, ...99-101

sodium in, ...77, 78 (table),

timing of consumption of, ...76

-recipe for: Homemade Sports Drink, .80

Sports foods, top, ...10 (table)

Sports nutritionists. *See* Dietitians

Starches. *See* Carbohydrates, complex; Grains; Pasta; Potatoes; Rice

Steamed vegetables, ...17

Stir-fried vegetables, ...18

Stomach:

    acid and upset, ...82-83, 91, 92

    cramping in, ... 90-91

    See also Digestion

Stress and dieting, ...45, 132-133

Stress fractures. *See* Bones

Sucrose. *See* Sugar

Sugar: 51

    as "evil", ...52

    daily intake of, ...15, 52

    mid-exercise consumption of, ...52, 95

    pre-exercise consumption of, ...52

    See also Blood sugar, low; Carbohydrates; Glycogen

Sugar and Spice Trail Mix, ... 88

Supplements:

    vitamin and mineral, ...40-46

    for weight gain, ...146-147

Sweating,

    fluid losses from, ... 76

    rate of, ...90

    replacing sodium losses from, ...78 (table), 100-101

    potassium losses in, ...78 (table)

    See also Dehydration

Sweets. *See* Junk foods; Snack foods; Sugar

Thirst, ...76

Timing of meals. See Meals, timing of

Tofu.   Diet, vegetarian

Training, pre-competition schedule for, ...107

Transit time. *See* Digestion

Traveling, ...114-119

    See also Breakfast; Dinner; Lunch; Snacking

Underweight. *See* Weight-gain diet

Urine and urination, ...76. 99

Urine Color Chart, ...76, 99

Vegetables: 17-19
     boosting intake of, ...14 (table)
     cooking methods for, ...17-19
     nutritional value of, ...10 (table)
     recommended intake, ... 12
Vegetarian diet. *See* Diet, vegetarian
Vitamin C (ascorbic acid): 43
     and iron absorption, ...62
Vitamin supplements. 40-46
     deficiency of, ...42
     sources of, ...12 (table)

Water:
     as fluid replacer, ...76, 79, 100
     See also Fluids; Recovery fluids
Websites, recommended:
     for vitamin information, ...46
     to resolve eating disorders. 142
Weight (body weight): 129, 138-139
     as a measure of fluid loss, ...76
     healthy, ...133
Weight-gain diet: 145-149
     rules for, ...146-148
     calories for, ...146
     foods for, ...147 (table)
Weight lifting, for muscle mass, ...146-147
Weight reduction: 126-134
     keys for successful, ...33, 130-133
     Weight-reduction (reducing) diet: 129
     caloric needs during, ... 24, 130-131
     hunger during, ...33, 10-131
     and dietary fat, ...132
     See also Body fat; Calories, estimating need for; Metabolism
Whole foods, ...44
Whole grains, ...26

Zinc: 43
     absorption of, ... 43
     boosting intake of, ...43 (table)
     recommended intake of, ... 43 (table)
     sources of, ...43 (table)

Photo and Illustration Credits:

Cover design and layout: Jens Vogelsang, Germany
Cover photos front: getty images, Polar Electro
Cover photos back: Polar Electro, Nancy Clark
Inside photos: getty images, imago sportfotodienst, Georg Neumann